MEMOS

from the

Stock Trader's Notebook

Ruling the Market From Mayhem to Mastery

Richard L. Smith

D1563620

For my gals: Ali and Adri

Introduction to The DVolT Advantage:

The Journey Begins.

You're holding a serious plan to improve stock market gains; a personal journey to enhanced investment results. I offer it not to advise you, but to show a different path you might consider as we proceed further into turbulent times. It is written for the shrewd investor intent on building wealth while tightly limiting risk. I demonstrate how you can change your attitude about investment decisions, how to structure stock charts and how to decide to make a trade. In simplest language possible, we specify what to watch, when to act, and why. We start with some theory and market observations, then discuss a few commonly-known investor tools and proceed into a street-smart discipline focused on market-beating profits and controlled loss. No options, day-trading or sophisticated trading instruments involved. The method is neither complicated nor difficult for the private investor to execute and is certainly simple to test and trade. It is original. It is real-world practical – and yes, I believe it can work for you. It has worked for me. There's little here on general investing or long term saving themes; this is a wise guy's tactical book – for the flinty-eyed trader who expects superior results.

As new risks of market turmoil emerge, the old stock market that was only interrupted from time to time by a couple of fearful panics is fading into history. More opportunities are out there to exploit, but maybe not with the dated popular investment theories of the past.... and certainly not if the stern lessons we should have learned in recent years are forgotten. Looking forward, we may not be able *to count on the Federal Reserve to rescue us from economic calamities or from the follies of political leaders often unfit for their responsibilities. Today's savvy investor, deluged by constant news headlines, may succeed with a different kind of focused clarity to make timely tactical choices.*

I want to especially thank those techno-wizards at yahoo.com and at thinkorswim.com from TDAmeritrade for providing us with simple-to-use analytic platforms small investors could once hardly imagine. Powerful tools are at hand – if we can only learn how to use them.

--- Richard Smith

"Do nothing."

"I beg your pardon?"

"When you have no move, you do nothing."

"He's under attack, Arnold!"

"All the more reason for patience. I've made my living, Mr. Thompson, in large part as a gambler. Some days I make twenty bets. Some days I make none. There are weeks, sometimes months, in fact, when I don't make a bet at all because there simply is no play. So I wait. Plan. Marshal my resources, and when I finally see an opportunity and there is a bet to make, I bet it all."

--Arnold Rothstein in Boardwalk Empire, Season Two

How Investors Go Wrong

You'll never have to search for new ways to screw up your investments. Always just ahead are a dozen easy-to-find pathways to your own personal stock market calamity. Whatever kind of investor you may be or whatever your education, opportunities to muck it up will find you if you let them. What can you say? It's the market. Stuff happens to the innocent and to the careless alike – so don't go looking for easy solutions. The lessons get expensive.

The first losers out of the gate are your passive-fearful worriers, too frightened of making mistakes to invest at all, or their opposites; the reckless active-indecisives who chase fads, headlines and internet rumor mills. Closely related are nervous fussbudgets who feel compelled to do something, to make a quick little trade to try to "fix" that worrisome MicroHard stock every time it makes a sudden zag when it was supposed to zig. Some losers can even convince themselves they've personally created a bull market rally merely by selling their last stock. It feels uncanny. Like a gift.

To our little collection of speculating mediocrities, we might add another colorful tribe, the highly credentialed stock market analysts, those professionals trained and paid to have opinions and offer them to the public like bread crumbs to pigeons. We must hope you're not among the dupes (dopes?) who have child-like faith in all the advice whooped through the daily media. If you are, your turn for a sour reckoning awaits you in good time. The elite analysts cipher and deduce far out of the public eye, somewhere in the fabled bowels of Goldman Sachs or Brown Brothers Harriman where the carpets are plush and the high floor office views inspiring. The B-Team stock barkers, the ones usually writing for the public (with a few exceptions), don't make predictions for the mere joys of helping us. Their true job, at which they excel, is to comment, to fill newsprint and networks with relentless bond and equity quacking and chatter. In flush markets and lean, in back offices or on broadcast sets, the show must go on. Working for retail brokerages, television programs and hedge funds as many do, bias may be written into almost any opinion you see or read in the media.

It's hardly a mystery when investment bank XYZ is pitching Microsoft for a big financial deal why its analysts don't dare publicly downgrade MSFT to so much as a "Hold". And speaking of deliberate inaccuracy, a great many big company earnings have been regularly beating analyst estimates in recent years. Now why might that be? Perhaps because analysts aren't rated just on their accuracy but also by what percentage of their "buy" recommendations actually climb in price. This leaves a juicy opportunity to game the system for your up-and-coming ledger readers. Any analyst worthy of his green eye shade knows the little investors (that's you and me, ma'am) will queue up like freaks at the methadone window to score shares of Consolidated Widgets when it crushes quarterly earnings estimates. So by simply predicting future earnings a tad lower than what he really expects, your garden-variety analyst has the opportunity to artificially pump up his success stats. Cute, yes?

Of course the one analyst everyone knows is Jim Cramer, who started his noise-banging shtick on the Mad Money TV show back in 2005. If he's turned thousands of viewers into millionaires I certainly haven't read about it. The program hasn't seemed to have worked so well for those poor souls prone to catching the vapors every time Jim slams his sell button. Still, Mad Money does seem preferable to watching the Youtube insomniac's cure, catching second-rate shills doing market infotainment for your wee-hours viewing pleasure. Smart and savvy as Cramer appears, I've always wanted to like the guy. He has a whale of a time doing his show, even if his wikipedia bio may seem troubling in spots. All in all, I think we're going to make you more gains in this book than a year of Mad Money rapid-fire opinions – and, as the bookies say, it ain't bragging if you can really do it.

A factoid: in good markets and bad, financial analysts for the retail trade routinely rate 40-50 % of all S&P500 companies as "buy", 40-50% as "hold" and fewer than 20% as "sell." Now if it occurs to you that it is mathematically unlikely for only about 15% to be lower than average, well, you're probably on to something. So go the sprinkles of half-truths or dated opinions doled out to the little people while investment bankers, board directors, executives and upper tier analysts gorge on obscene gains and incomes. Statista.com reports the CEO-to-worker compensation ratio in top publicly-traded companies soared from 24.3 in 1970 to 670 in 2022.

So they pull far ahead in wealth, and here we are.

-----------------------.

MEMO from *The Stock Trader's Notebook*:

Look, I hate to bore you with my little speech, but if I don't, my lawyer will beat me like a broken drum. So here goes: Nothing in this book is intended as investment advice, OK? Not a word of it. I'm not a certified financial advisor or CPA or broker or anyone who tapdances on the sunny side of financial regulations. I'm an experienced private investor who will discuss a method that works for me. This book describes my private thinking and my personal journey, a narrative of ideas you may want to consider. That's all. (Heck, I've been wrong before.) So we'll say it again, Gwen -- do not think this book offers any financial or investing advice. It doesn't. (Can we please proceed now? Good.)

-------------------.

On October 29, 2022 the Wall Street Journal ran a major article in their Saturday edition: *Where Are Markets Headed? Six Pros Take Their Best Guess* and, sure enough, their opinions were all over the place. To paraphrase; *The market hadn't seen its bottom, but Blankfein sees "silver linings" ..., be brave in your decisions.... we're undergoing a structural shift,... I see volatility ahead..... Bonds are an opportunity.... But there'll be more inflation ahead.*

It's a tried and true format, constantly repeated: lure a gaggle of prominent investing pros together, let them have at each other, and then publish their conversation. Sells a ton of newspapers and garners lots of clicks. Just how the small investor reaches actionable conclusions from such a hash of expert chatter goes unmentioned. Exactly which advice do you take when opinions of the pros are vague or off topic or contradictory or urge you to "be brave"? When we're done and dumbfounded, the road ahead is hardly clearer. One reason why I remain with Merrill Lynch is they are one of those brokerages who regularly publish investment bulletins to their clients with specific advice of "buy this / avoid that". Mother Merrill may be wrong at times, but she's not vague.

Analyst opinions apart, we don't much understand how our own personalities incline us to settle on an investing style. Nor do we know how our habits are unconsciously driven, but we can suspect that many of our investment choices are less cerebral/logical than we might believe. You could suppose that younger, more confident investors might be quicker on the trigger than the retired geezer nursing his nest egg, but that's not explaining much. If you were to ask a used car buyer why he was looking at Fords and not Hondas he'd give you his reasons. Though his claims of Ford superiority could have some merit, they probably don't fully explain why he has nixed Hondas. After all the logical reasons have been explored, marketing experts would know there is almost always some hazy <u>something</u> about used Fords which that particular auto buyer likes.

In an anxious age when people have fewer friends and are not so associated with social organizations or whose family members are far-flung, many customers want to feel an affinity with the companies they patronize. Apple, Starbucks, Ben & Jerry and Whole Foods are four companies that have successfully capitalized on that need. People want to feel connected and will sometimes pay premium prices for that feeling. It seems just possible those subtle yearnings to belong may also extend to what stocks attract people. Unlike an investor in equities, the typical used car buyer is often limited to what autos happen to be available for sale nearby. But a practically unlimited choice of stocks and funds an investor might own makes personal inclinations to pick one stock over three thousand others more difficult to understand. Down the road we'll be talking a lot more about the dangers of "feel-good investing" and our emotions and inclinations quietly leading us toward some cars (or stocks!) and away from others.

Finally, you have the oddest failure-prone under-achievers of all; the serenely self-assured, the cocky-confident investors who have settled – by one means or another – on a couple of notions and cannot be budged by logic, arithmetic or earthquake. This stolid bunch are curiously incurious about the fog of markets or future events, satisfied in their opinions, smug in their perspicacity and convinced they are better clued in than naive rubes like us. These poor doomed chaps bring a kind of fatal arrogance to the market. If you have ever been trapped at a party by some blowhard lecturing you on his politics, his investments, or reasons why his kids are smarter and cuter than yours in every way, you know the type. "Stay-the-course!" is his odd mantra and self-confidence is his undoing.

So take heart. Chances are excellent this windbag will one day take hair-curling investment losses. Some are too arrogant to reflect and question their own judgment. Others fall back on cynical resignation; *It's all rigged! You can't beat this market!* But the highest bluster of *"no-you-can't"* rants blossom brightest when you tell them you have found success and portfolio growth by trading equities according to a simple, disciplined method.

No you can't?

Yes you can.

You can do this. You can out-Warren any Buffett you're ever apt to meet. It's not nuclear physics or instinct or dumb luck.

Investing and trading success can follow when you jettison your hunches, disregard news headlines, and focus your attention on a small and clearly defined set of stocks and market data – and then act promptly when the probabilities veer in your favor. This book is a road map for you to consider, a simple little system – as nuts-and-bolts and as just-follow-the-damn-dots as I can make it.

And of course, right off, here <u>they</u> come now. All those doubts and suspicions do have their way of springing up, right on cue. Here's one for you -- *"Well if your big idea is so great, wise guy, how come everyone isn't doing it?"* Good question. We'll get to that – in detail – just as soon as we lay out the method, the whys and the whens.

The skeptical reader remains doubtful, of course. If granny used to say – *Fine words butter no parsnips*, we reply – *Suspicions don't pay stock dividends.* This book isn't about to lead you around with hints and gas-bag notions, just to wind up at some vague, theoretical nowhere a hundred pages later. We're going to dive right into the heart of our method, and show you step-by-step how it does work in real-world investing. So hold onto to those doubts. While we walk you through the prelims, I'll try to anticipate and answer every objection you might have.

That said, skepticism is the healthiest attitude you can bring to the table, Mable. I hope you take nothing in this book – or from any investment notion – at face value. You could do worse than to borrow a page from journalism school to vow, "If mother says she loves you, check it out." Once we run through the theory and the brass-tacks practicalities of actually trading the method, I'm going to insist you test and test to see how it would have worked during different periods in the past as well as to paper-trade to prove to yourself how it actually works in the real-world present. ***I don't want you to risk a dime until you have built your own self confidence from personal testing and paper-trading experience.*** I hope you will do this in all kinds of markets and in different sectors. Tests are simple to do and require you to only keep some careful notes from a few basic stock charts I show you how to create.

What Not To Expect

In case you're wondering – the answer is no, Flo. This isn't another day-trading scheme dressed up to look sober. It's not some crypto currency angle or on-line gambling code or implied volatility options formula or high-wire-act-for-suckers trick. I'm not selling some online "service". We're not going to work the headlines or sleuth out analyst recommendations. There's no magic-bullet analytic short-cut gizmo in here or so-called super-cash generator, nor arbitrage scheme. No bird dogging inside buyers or following a calendar, trying to chase ex-dividend days one stock after another. And we're certainly not going to leverage you up and increase your risk to inflate dividends. That's as dead as disco.

None of it. And no futures or FOREX either, OK?

What we <u>are</u> going to do is improve performance by specializing in a few specific assets – clearly defined securities, mind you – where we can make high-probability trades. We zero in on those – right where there's a better-than-even opportunity to anticipate future stock or fund trends. Equally important, we pre-plan what actions to take when we are wrong. Our plan allows for surprises, for the unforeseen, even the unimagined risks. It may sound complicated, but our strategy is deceptively simple. We'll lay the principles out in such elementary style even rookies will pick up the rules and apply them. Of course, that means we'll cover some basics already known to experienced investors – but if you market-scarred veterans will stick with me here, I think even you will be well rewarded.

------------------.

MEMO from *The Stock Trader's Notebook:* "Everyone has a plan 'til they get punched in the mouth." **--Mike Tyson**

------------------.

You're not always going to make a good choice, Joyce. But when you do stumble and are wrong more often than you hoped, you'll still make excellent gains over time. You may well ask, "What if the plan doesn't work?" The answer, we expect our efforts to sometimes go awry. This market <u>will</u> turn against you. Wrong moves are built in. They are inevitable even --- and still we will succeed because over time your profitable investments will consistently tend to be more frequent and larger than your losses.

And face it. For some of you frowning skeptics, this could be it, guys. This might be your best chance to make good if your life's hit some potholes. Maybe you struggled in college, or you never went at all. Maybe you're doing OK but feel inflation gaining on you. Maybe others were promoted past you. We all have those chances to forget the appointment, lose the wallet or miss the 5:23 to Poughkeepsie ... or for some of us the career's Big Oppty might never have come at all. Maybe one did pass by, but you didn't see it. And there's no accounting for plain ol' bad luck.

So if any part of that sounds like a dark little chapter in your personal bio, I hope you won't let the told-you-so crowd say you never rallied. Because I believe this IS your opportunity. If you're ready for a come-back, we will work with a goal of starting to make some money; a lot of it. Maybe you've done well but hope to do better. Maybe you have never really invested (or you tried and blew it) and you fret like the lost cat who wandered into a dog pound at the thought of losing more. Well, junior, time to hike up those whitey-tighties and work for some gains.

----------------------.

MEMO from *The Stock Trader's Notebook:*

If you truly are a raw rookie, a toddling tyro in the high weeds,

a green-to-the-gills beginner when it comes to investing, wealth management, planning, savings for retirement, this is the <u>second</u> book you should be reading. If you're a little fuzzy about 401k, term life insurance, mortgage deductions, IRAs, I-Bonds, mutual funds and compound interest, drop everything and go fetch yourself an updated copy of "<u>The Only Investment Guide You'll Ever Need</u>" by Andrew Tobias. He and Suze Orman ("<u>The 9 Steps To Financial Freedom</u>" and "<u>The Road To Wealth</u>") have already covered saving for retirement, budgeting and long term goals, and they've done it very well.

This is more a book for determined and ambitious investors, about aggressive growth at reduced risk. This is a wise guy's book – for trading people who demand results.

--------------------.

First Step: Fix your 'tude, dude

OK. Right to business now. We start with a challenge, just one little question: *How badly do you want to become a successful investor? I mean, y'know, REALLY?*

Would you change your routine for twenty minutes a day?

"Well, uh," you might say. "I'm pretty jammed up with the job and the kids and all. I might forget sometimes."

OK then, could you commit to twenty minutes a week?

"Oh, that's easy," you might say, "I could probably do that – if I knew the change was worth the effort!"

All right, we're getting somewhere.

Now how about this: Say you're a Dallas Cowboys fan and I come to you with a wild-eyed, crazy offer. I say: "*I can make you a successful investor if you totally reject the Cowboys and become a big Philadelphia Eagles fanatic.*" Would you do it?

"<u>WHAT</u> the …..?"

Hold on, Leon. Can you answer the question? Speechless ? What would you do?

All right. Let's try one last question.. *If the only way you could become a skilled investor was by ditching the Democrat Party and voting Republican for the rest of your life (or vice versa) what would you say?*

"Oh, that's ridiculous!"

Well, of course it is. But see my point here. I want you to look at your attitudes to recognize how stubborn you are in your preferences and beliefs. The idea of change seems unthinkable to most people, especially when there's no clear link between the change and the desired benefit. When it comes to money and investing (not to mention politics, sex or football) we have already settled into firm preferences. The average jake or jane has become comfortable within their own areas of opinions and can hardly be persuaded to push beyond those closed borders. So that's the first problem you need to face. I don't ask you to believe anything – I only ask that you read and proceed <u>as if</u> you could rely on the trading system – but not invest a dollar. Keep your doubts intact, but put them temporarily aside until you've seen the entire protocol. While some new investors may be tentatively ready to consider new information and investment tactics, I'm sure many veterans have already made up their minds and will hardly consider a different method unless to debunk it out of hand.

So let's not sugar-coat it. Here it is straight, Kate. Your fears, your ego and your rigidity are your first problems because you're going to see that with this system investing success requires you to get a grip on your opinions and your emotions. I really can make you a better investor/trader, but you're going to need a small, serious attitude adjustment. You'll have to accept a couple of procedures you've never done before. You must say good-bye to stocks and funds you've invested in for years and work with some others you might never have thought about. **<u>The more cocky-confident you are in your opinions, the worse you will do.</u>** Mastering the simple, basic tactics in this book will be a personal journey. It will be a challenge, and for you arrogant know-it-alls out there, it's a waste of time. Look, no offense, but we really must push ourselves beyond talk about the kinds of investments you like to do or what feels right or what investments make you comfortable. Investing isn't back rubs.

Remember that. Let's move on.

You may think me presumptuous in my demands. (I think that way myself sometimes.) But I do have decades of investing experience and I've made a point of not letting life's lessons go to waste. After a little pension, I make an excellent living like <u>you</u> want to: investing and trading the market. And at long last, I'm good at it. I have probably been trading far longer than you. And sure, my record had its ups and downs. (Has it ever!) Maybe you'll recognize the old feeling. Market goes up and I'm just bustin' with confidence. Market collapses, like it did in '08, and Hare Krishna starts looking like a career option. Thump a little drum. Hop about in the park. The full Monty. And the wife – well, the woman has no interest in the market whatever – if my wife saw something on the news and at dinner happened to ask how we were doing, I used to mumble something – or I'd just lie. (That was when we were first married. She's on to me now. She checks the brokerage accounts.) Whatever "la problema," when a guy has married a mile out of his league to a pretty younger Latina who grew up dirt poor on her daddy's Colombian coffee plantation, nothing lights happy smiles like "Let's go shopping." A cheap ploy, perhaps, but it works every time.

For my part, I've always tried to live more simply than I could afford. To my daughter's exasperation, I still keep my ancient 2001 Honda for trips to the mountains and grocery runs to Aldi or Walmart. I'm a Costco kinda guy kept by two Bloomingdale's gals. Still, we get on happily.. Growing older, my wife and I have found other satisfactions in making the lives of people we love more comfortable. We have had long and lavish European river cruises. My daughter had a free ride all through Penn State, something I thought was the minimum necessary I had to do to look myself in the mirror. After she graduated and struggled financially in her first job, my wife and I were able to buy her a cute little condo in downtown Philadelphia on the sly and throw her a surprise Christmas party, giving her the front door key on a pretty red bow. We changed her life and never regretted it for a minute.

Every one of my wife's Colombian nieces and nephews knows to expect a monthly Western Union remittance for as long as they stay in university. One nephew dropped out of engineering school to devote himself to his rock band. We pleaded with him to stay in school and argued there's no shame if engineering was too rough a course for him. The world is full of guys who dropped out of E-school and went on to be successful elsewhere. We said we'd be glad to help if he wanted to start again in something different. He turned us down and now serves as an example to his cousins what's apt to happen when you face life in South America without a skill or you cross Aunt Adriana's iron determination to shoe-horn her family into the Colombian upper middle class. I do feel badly for him. I imagine what's tons of fun in a going-nowhere band at 22 gets tired around age 30. He probably already feels he's too old to start again. Even with money and the best of intentions, some stories just don't end well.

---------------.

Money will not buy happiness, but it will let you be unhappy in nice places.

~ W. C. Fields

--------------.

So if money won't always bring happiness, it certainly can offer a kind of liberty to put you in control of your own time, free to spend your days as you please. Sartre wrote, "Hell is other people" and with enough extra coming in, you might free yourself from life's dismal jobs, debts, rough edges and rougher characters. They can all be .... gone. As for marriage and money, there appears to be a strong inverse correlation between money and divorce. The percentage of marital breakups decreases sharply and steadily as household income increases from zero to about $200,000, and thereafter seems to level off, according to flowingdata.com. Since money problems are a major cause of marital discord, one might expect that with affluence, couples lose at least one important reason to quarrel. Think of the dishware you can save when cups and soup bowls aren't thrown around in the kitchen any more.

----------------.

MEMO from *The Stock Trader's Notebook:* Can money make you happy? Of course it can! But does it? You can use behavioral finance concepts to spend your money in ways that increase your happiness. (1) Buy experiences, not things. (2) Buy many small things instead of few big ones. (3) Pay now to consume later. (4) Help others.

— John R Nofsinger, <u>The Psychology of Investing</u>

--------------.

Still, life on a tight budget might have its good points. If you're inclined toward vice or addiction, sometimes poverty and responsibilities can act as a crude set of brakes on harmful habits; maybe not enough to save you, but enough to slow you down. The first time I ever heard of the fentanyl drug was reading the news reports that the pop singer Michael Jackson had managed to kill himself on it. It's downright dangerous to be a young rock star or big rap artist. We all know it; with enough youth, success and fame often comes a long enough leash to be as drunk, vicious, or reckless as you like.

Even through my numbskull years, those late teens and early twenties, I was never cool enough to be big into sin. I was certainly tempted and, yes, was guilty of things that fell into my lap, as they say – by accident. But I was too insecure; not to mention too clumsy even to properly deal out a deck of cards and too dumb to understand I was borderline poor. My two salvations all those trying-and-struggling years were steady work and constant investment reading and self-questioning. I was determined not to repeat my early mistakes (like that disastrous divorce) and was not going to be lulled by the cookie-cutter advice of the big brokerages. Of course for a long time my book learning made zip difference where it really counted; how the portfolio was growing. Despite everything, after all the self-help investment books I pored over, my performance was, you know ... meh.

That changed when some loose thoughts slowly gelled and I

could put together a stock-trading protocol that focused on fewer tightly defined areas – and see the process actually evolve and perform in different markets. The closer I followed the theory as it developed, the better I did. After a while I could see I was out-doing the market. My portfolio grew when the S&P500 went up. It steadied when the market slumped. It grew again when stocks seemed to have no direction at all. When I wandered off the reservation to try something different, progress stalled. Eventually I got it. And I'm still improving all the time.

I took a good long while to begin writing about it. With my largely self-taught investment skills, I still hesitate to express opinions on how to deploy money. I knew of dumpsters behind libraries and book stores from Bangor to Oahu loaded with old useless stock market books no one wanted. I didn't want to write more "sounds-good-but-won't-really-work" trash-bound, unrealistic vanity pap destined for the discount bin, but I really do think I have something worth the read here. I was getting up mornings so jazzed about every new market day that I couldn't wait to write about it.

My method is original, I think, but anyone would have to be terminally naive to think he's come up with something really new in this market. I know there has been ample discussion and even exchange traded funds devoted to low volatility stocks, which are cousins to what we will be doing, but they are not nearly so tightly defined as the choices we will focus on. I think there are probably guys out there quietly trading something like my process (there MUST be!) only maybe they never thought of it as a particular discipline or they didn't think to put all the parts together, or never thought about the method as a complete protocol. Or maybe they're just too crafty to drop their towel. Despite all my reading over the years, I've never come across anyone who has tried to distill it all together and discuss anything close to the method in its entirety.

---------------.

Formal education will make you a living; self-education will make you a fortune.

- Jim Rohn

.---------------.

One good thing about the system is that it will take only a few minutes to monitor. In fact, if you really don't like fiddling about in the market, you don't need to check a few assets more than say, two or three times a week or so .... and I've even worked out the steps for people who can't bear to look at their portfolio more than once or twice a month. And when I say it is easy, well, you probably won't really believe me there either. Dancing the charleston, learning French, or playing piano can seem easy for people who have a knack for them. Most of us just muddle through, if we make the attempt at all. But this really is easy. Just hold onto your doubts and stay with me a little while here. Judge me on what you learn. I think you'll say, "Y'know, this makes sense. I really CAN do it."

"OBJECTION! I bet you're going to slop up some hog wash gizmo formula you tack onto low volatility stocks you claim works for YOU, but won't work for anyone else who tries it in the real world. You're about to roll out some "sure thing" theory with spreads or shorting or some scheme that sort of works on paper. Maybe there's some weirdo candlestick chart formations mumbo-jumbo, or algebraic ratios or widgets-and-commodities arbitrage nonsense up your sleeve. Well, save your breath, Bubba. I don't believe a word of it."

ANSWER: Not a bit. I won't propose a single idea that a kid couldn't easily understand. We will always seek clarity, simplicity and discipline. You're really going to get this. In fact, you might slap your forehead and ask, "Why didn't I think of it before?" And I can promise it's not a procedure you already know about, tarted up with a couple of fancy ribbons.

------------------.

You may be a veteran investor who thinks he forgot more about trading than anybody else knows, or maybe you're some young stud with an itch, some wanna-be Soros in Birkenstocks casting voo-doo chicken bones for favorable options spreads. Both will probably find a better technique here. Experienced investors with real knowledge will find a new perspective to hone those skills and supplement their best tactics, but rookies still on page seventeen of their Stocks For Dummies book will find a guide to help them enter into trading – carefully and successfully. If you're some college sophomore who's caught the stock market bug from that big-talking crowd of day traders yukking it up down the dormitory hall, you really should read this. You've certainly heard some chest-thumping booyahs from the upper bunks, I'll bet. But did you hear about the guys who went bust? I mean, c'mon, Brucie. What do you really think happens to coked-up nimrods who trade on social media tips? Think your Twitter and Facebook howlers are good investment advisors? Let's not even commence.

Before we proceed further, I want to add a couple of words to nervous investors; those inexperienced people sensibly frightened of losing money. Every step of the way we are going to be especially careful to manage and limit your market risks. Avoidance of big losses is at the heart of what we do. We'll talk more about risk-management later, so take a breath here. I intend to start you out very carefully. I'm not going to suggest anything flashy or speculative like start-ups or penny stocks. Like the dot.com explosion of the 1990s, and all the investment promises of legalizing marijuana and EV subsidies, there are fortunes to be made for some early speculators. But a lot of secondary buyers get butchered. (Happens every time.) We're still in the early acts with stuff like AI, fusion, battery technology and green energy. It's going to be interesting to see how they shake out for investors, but for the moment, they are long-shot speculations. We don't deal with long shots. We work by finding probabilities … one after another while we ignore the stock shills croaking their chorus like bullfrogs on a log. If the show must go on, we're not obligated to tune in.

---------------.

MEMO from *The Stock Trader's Notebook:* <u>Uh oh</u> ..... **A major study by** S. Siegel of Arizona State University and H. Cronqvist, **using the Swedish Twins Registry (the largest such registry in the world) compared investment habits of identical twins who shared the same genes to fraternal twins and concluded that education may cause you to change habits destructive to your health, but learning has little or no effect on improving your investment habits. They state** *<u>We find no evidence that education is a significant moderator of genetic investment behavior.</u>*

(Siegel and Cronqvist seem to be saying that stock market advice books and courses won't help you be a better investor. If our method is successful for you, we have to show them wrong!)

---------------------.

THE EXTERNAL PROBLEM: Like poker, investing is a game of incomplete knowledge. (Except poker is harder. And more fun.)

It's a big market of smart people you're up against. We can only guess what the captains of commerce and poo-bahs of profit are thinking. All across corporate America, in city canyons and commercial campuses, decisions are made. Assets are deployed. Staffs hired, trained, transferred, terminated. Bonds are floated. Buyouts, buy-backs, IPOs announced. Sales, revenues and costs are reported and projected. Floods of data flow. Accounting and legal departments collect, write, edit and publish. Each announcement joins the information flowing by.

And how do we keep up with this information river? We can't even begin, Flynn.

Most of us don't have a clue what was discussed by the sultans of sales in Microsoft or Oracle this morning. And those NATO talks about selling big new weapons systems to Europe – who is going to get a big surprise contract? Which companies are about to sign a massive new multi-year agreement next week and who knows about it BEFORE the reports are published?

Not us, Gus. We can hardly imagine what is brewing in the corner suites until well after it happens, but we compete with wise guys who do know. To them, we're a couple of rubes pressing noses against the glass who couldn't bribe our way into the executive elevator. Even when important new data is published only a few of us spot it in the flood of other information tumbling past.

Whatever important facts you learn, the big money guys, the "connected" guys learned it before you had a fighting chance. With wrist-slap penalties for illegal trades or iffy reporting, in early October 2022 businessinsider.com found some 72 congressmen guilty of stock trading irregularities. Yet the legislature managed to postpone voting on a new law until after the November 2022 mid terms when many figured it would likely die a quiet death in the post-election hub-bub. Time.com wrote, "To say the bill is weak, however, would be an understatement. The bill is dangerous. It would undermine what little ethics we have in our federal government."

Looking into government corruption is like opening a jar and watching the snakes slither out – more rattlers and copperheads than could possibly fit, yet they just keep coming. And whatever tips or perks they get, it never seems to be quite enough. In July 2022 Alexandria Ocasio-Cortez broke her progressive poster-gal cover to wail it was summertime and the living was sleazy on a mere congresswoman's salary. Yet they all seem to retire wealthy. The last time congress made a meaningful effort to curb insider trading abuses was in passing the hilariously named "Stop Trading on Congressional Knowledge Act" back in 2012.

---------------.

"When they call the roll in the Senate, the senators do not know whether to answer 'Present' or 'Not Guilty'."

— **Theodore Roosevelt**

----------------.

"As Covid Hit, Washington Officials Traded Stocks With Exquisite Timing"

--Wall Street Journal Front Page Headline, Oct 19, 2022

------------------.

So it goes, and so far we've touched only on elected representatives. There are bureaucratic herds of appointed officials of all stripes and pay levels also snorting at the trough of early information. You and I can just suck rocks waiting for an honest investment environment and distract ourselves with sordid histories of self-dealing in high places. The bottom line is we won't know important new information until after the "early whispers" have been passed out among the favored few via office chat or pillow-talk. We get the stale leftovers, the second-hand skinny. So give it up. Unless we're favorably positioned in life, we aren't going to get far trying to find better information. That's the bad news.

The good news is we can work around all that.

A Little Deeper Now – The Inner Problem

------------------.

".... two important facts about our minds: we can be blind to the obvious, and we are also blind to our blindness." --- from **THINKING FAST AND SLOW, Daniel Kahneman**

--------------------.

Maybe the best investment book I ever read was, *The Money Game* by Adam Smith. On the first page he writes, "This is a book about image and reality and identity and anxiety and money," and Smith speaks of the crippling emotions that individuals carry into their investing. The first time I read those opening paragraphs I wanted to pound the table, and shout, "Yes! DAMN straight!" For a long time I also wondered about what kind of unholy grip our twisted biases and feelings play upon our investment choices.

I have participated in on-line investment forums for years (mostly under the handles *richardsok, rokstar* or *sokky*) and I routinely see people passionately committed to their opinions. Some never take a break from airing their egos. Others erupt into mockery or abuse when someone tries to refute their notions. In some forums the problem gets so bad members have to appoint a referee to enforce the rules with the power to blackball repeat offenders. Other than a few serious discussion sites, the cage-match atmosphere of investment chat rooms typically degenerates into a kind of free-for-all without even the pretense of an exchange of ideas. They're not really quarreling to make a profit, these guys. It's not money they fuss over in their keyboard hissy-fits. They want to be right. They want to be affirmed, to be admired. And yes, many times they just want to humiliate someone. (And here you thought you'd outgrown the junior high lunchroom.) A colossal waste of your attention most of it Is, too. Those are the conversations outsiders like us are privy to in real time – and they're indicative of the level of thought that generally goes into small investor stock picks. It's entertaining to read but generally worthless.

So we have some idea how the little investors can think, but roughly nothing of today's conversations in executive offices – and we have to know equally little about the internal attractions, those emotional whys of our own thought habits in investments and in our lives. I still wonder how so many smart people can screw up their lives. What is in us that we pick lovers and spouses who turn out to be horrid for us, or we selfish and quarrelsome with them and proceed to bring out the worst in each other? Well, choices we make in the stock market can be just as damaging. In marriage, you start down a rosy path and wreck your personal life. In the stock market bright people keep repeating the same blunders, and have little idea how they winnow down their hunches to pick an investment that turns out to be among the worst. Investors may insist they choose purely on the news or from stock analysis, but most of us can't fathom what mental gears are really whirring about inside that size seven, luring us to some stocks and not to others.

----------------.

MEMO from *The Stock Trader's Notebook:* There are known knowns. These are the things we know we know. There are known unknowns. There are things we know we don't know. But there are also unknown unknowns. There are things we don't know we don't know.

--Donald Rumsfeld

-----------------.

Don't think we're going to learn much about the little landmines laying in your own odd-thinking habits. This is not that kind of book. It's been said humanity is made of twisted timber, so we need to understand that our stock choices are influenced by unconscious biases rooted in the deeply personal, if not irrational. You're not going to cure your personal tics today, Ray. But if we are to be successful traders, somehow we must find a technique to work around those barely understood druthers and wants. The Optimized Portfolio website lists twenty three different investing biases, any one of them capable of chewing through your portfolio like a pack of rabid mandrills, leaving you with the scraps and tatters …. And wondering just what you did wrong.

Some of us are rapid-fire traders churning our accounts continuously. Others proceed like they need an act of congress to buy five shares of General Motors. But no successful investor should either enjoy or dislike to trade. I argue you should buy a security when you see a probability it is going to climb, whether that opportunity appears twice a week or twice a year. If someone with a gambling itch actually enjoys buying and selling, then speculating has become for him a pleasurable pastime – a fun hobby bringing with it a gambler's "buzz" – and, to tell the truth, possible danger. In the end, I will argue that feelings should be irrelevant. We should trade out of an asset when the probabilities appear against us. Always then but only then.

Since opinions and hunches can be wildly unreliable, our goal is to steer away from the high weeds of feelings and emotion and toward a clear path of objective data-based decisions. But what data? Didn't we just establish that TV news and websites were part of the problem? Didn't we just remark that the newest, most valuable information is difficult to locate and use? We certainly did, and that is why we will put aside the daily information deluge and replace it with a couple of simple markers that point our way ahead like signposts in a fog.

Maybe you're a confident investor because you're one of many whose portfolio has grown over the years. Well let's not mistake bull markets for brains. All investors should have seen their wealth grow mightily the past couple of decades. Since the mid 1980s we've only lived through the greatest bull market climbs in history. But the low-hanging fruit of long rallies and a compliant Federal Reserve may be in our rear view mirror. Any wise guy knows a trader's constant question is always, "NOW what?"

And just now there's precious little to suggest that our way forward will be anywhere as rosy as the good old days. In the mid-2020s decade and beyond, investors will seek to invest profitably in an economic environment far different – and maybe much uglier than the past. A tiny fifteen cent baggie of McDonald's fries now costs 2.39. The president assures us the economy is sensational, tells us inflation is at zero and proceeds to drain the Strategic Petroleum Reserve while Vladimir Putin helped to put "dirty bomb" back on junior high school vocabulary lists. If you look at today's global economies; the shortages, the inflation, the diseases, the unimaginable ocean of debts and obligations, not to mention the wars, the myopia of our corrupt and pandering ruling class – you might decide the easy money has already been made. And I might agree with you. Long gone are the days one might just park $20,000 into Apple or Microsoft stock and forget about money worries forever. We're going to need a new way of investment thinking for a different and anxious future.

Back to the Charts ..... But why ?

"They're useless! Stock charts just look backwards. It's like driving your car looking into the rear-view mirror." You hear that once in a while, but when the lecture ends we all return to our charts anyway, searching for patterns which (we hope!) give us clues how a security will behave in the future. Studying a chart is like following animal tracks in the snow; a recent history of events, even maybe a pattern of personality; where the beast has headed and where and when it changed direction.

A chart's predictive powers seem to often have an inverse relationship to the strength of the observer's opinions. The perpetual danger in chart reading is the risk of seeing what we want to see, like inkblots, and I suspect it's a comfort – often a baseless one – to "recognize" a pattern where a stock has traded the last few months. We may have the illusion of information or we fantasize conclusions about the future from the impressions about the past that a stock chart gives us. Are the stars written in charts with recognizable shapes? Is there reliable meaning in pennants, engulphing vectors or double bottoms? And those candlestick charts – do fame and wealth await those who study the arcane subtleties they seem to whisper?

Probably not. Nevertheless there are a few basic chart patterns that do give valid hints toward the immediate future. For instance, there's the old saying, "Never catch a falling knife." Everyone knows it because it's true. Your chances of success in buying a steadily-falling stock are undeniably slim, just as the chances are fairly good that a stock hitting a new high will probably go on for at least a while longer to hit more new highs.... until the happy trend inevitably ends.

But few of us are satisfied with the simple A-B-Cs of chart use. Some believe there may be profound and useful investing truths to be found, venturing deeper into head-and-shoulder or cup-and-handle formations and the like. How many times have you read something like, *"If XYZ's recent double bottom holds, we may see a relief rally, but if the price breaks through support, then we are possibly facing a renewed bear trend."* In plain English, this is like saying, *"If XYZ goes down it will probably go down, but if it doesn't go down it might go up."* The financial news, TV and print, is full of straight-faced nonsense like this, and we consume it. More fools us.

We're going to use charts in our method, but with a difference. We're not only interested in <u>what</u> a stock has done but in <u>how</u> the stock has behaved. We suggest a chart's predicting reliability depends very much on what stock or fund we are charting, leading us to the rather curious claim (and you may demand a lot of evidence to accept it) *not all stocks and funds lend themselves equally to chart analysis.* It sounds ridiculous to say, but we will be as interested in a stock's "chart personality" as we are in its history.

It may be a stretch to suggest different companies have different personalities that would affect our wish to invest in them – but we have known for a long time that some crowds have moods and personalities distinct from other crowds and also different from the individuals that comprise those crowds. Take 70,000 undergrads and alums at a USC-Notre Dame game and you'll see quite a different personality than a middle aged alumna sitting alone by herself in the stands. While it may be marginally true that the executives and customers of, say, a retail department store might have different personality types than minerals & mining executives and buyers, for our purposes it is more relevant to note that, as a group, the <u>investors</u> in various companies might be distinguished from the investors in others. People who own Tesla are apt to be somewhat different than the folks holding Toll Bros. stock, who can probably be distinguished from people watching Union Pacific –

and those small differences may be reflected in the character and movements of their charts. We might even venture to theorize that the aggregate group personalities of some investor groups could create "chart personalities" that can be distinguished from others. Whether true or not, we certainly know different stock charts have different volatilities and behaviors.

If we suspect this may be true, how might we test it? How to examine it? How might we use it?

------------------.

Remember, your goal in investing isn't to earn average returns; you want to do better than average. Thus, your thinking has to be better than that of others – both more powerful and at a higher level. Since other investors may be smart, well informed and highly computerized, you must find an edge they don't have. You must think of something they haven't thought of, see things they miss, or bring insight they don't possess. You have to react differently and behave differently.

--Howard Marks "I Beg To Differ"

------------------.

Game Time At Last: Not Just Low Volatility, but Deep Volatility

Imagine you're watching a flea make two hops to the left followed by one hop to the right. OK, what does that tell you about predicting its next hop, the fourth hop? Nothing, of course. You can't predict a flea's next move after a couple of jumps. A flea makes volatile and random moves for reasons impossible for the casual observer to predict.

Very good. Now picture a second image. You are in a balloon, watching a large cargo ship below, moving due east. After a little while you notice it just begins to turn to starboard. You can even see its wake "bend" as it starts to head a bit southerly. OK, now, what can you predict about the ship's future direction for the next half hour or so? Clearly, it is likely the ship will continue its turn to its right, charting a more southward course. Exactly where that final direction lies, you don't know -- but it is probable the future direction will not be due east or north.

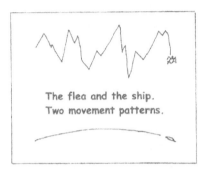

The flea and the ship.
Two movement patterns.

Remember this. The ship turns in a very low volatility manner, more calmly and predictably than the flea.

Perhaps you can sense where I'm heading. At the start of our system we attempt to *confine ourselves to those few stocks and funds with histories of exceptionally low volatility, what we might call DEEP VOLATILITY chart movements.* We comb the market to find assets with stock charts that tend to move like an ocean ship on a calm sea and not like most stocks move – like fleas in the sunshine. Think of a patch of ocean in a stiff breeze with its choppy random waves, sharp peaks and currents. Now picture the same body of water after you've spilled a gallon of oil on it. The wave action persists, but in greatly softened manner. Gone are the sharp-edged peaks, the choppy, volatile waves. They are replaced with low-rolling swells and gentle wavelets, even though the same forces; the same winds and currents are still at play. We are going to concentrate on any asset with a similar history, an established pattern that begins most of its upturns slowly, giving us the opportunity to buy a position just as it is starting to rise. Similarly, we will search for those tending to fall slowly – a stock we can sell early – frequently before terrible drops -- so we can limit our losses.

_____.

Right about here I can picture a hundred veteran readers sputtering, *"Hey, dummy! Just because your stock has started to rise, that's no promise it won't fall right back down again!"* **That's right – and we'll address that a couple pages ahead. Just stay with me a bit more, Lenore.**

----------.

In broad terms, I'm suggesting that the lowest volatility stocks, or "ocean liner stocks," or "oil-on-water-stocks" if you will, help you make better predictions on future movements than "flea stocks".

Unfortunately, "flea pattern" stocks out-number true "oil-on-water" stocks by oh, about two hundred-to-one.

Here we might confront the popular orthodox counter claim: that over the course of its history, the Dow Jones Industrial Average has always recovered from bear markets and has climbed even higher, so the best tactic for your average investor is to simply buy and hold. Millions of investors believe in this theory like they believe in gravity and I certainly don't expect to convince them otherwise. But this is the moment I was referring to when I asked you to open your mind and stretch your thinking.

Sure, the stock market has climbed greatly over the past decades, and for millions who have never paid attention to markets, just adding a few more dollars monthly into an equity fund has worked marvelously well. As the market soared over the past half century, it practically turned into another background theme of the boomer generation – one of the things we all shared, like Woodstock, Princess Diana, Reagan and 9/11. Just as your grand daddy used to talk about the power of compound interest – when banks actually paid interest – now we talk about the power of continuously buying and holding stocks over the course of decades.

But even the long trends do not trend indefinitely, and stocks have not risen smoothly. There were periods when the market gave us a taste of the whip to fall and continue falling. The 1970s and early 1980s were a particularly sad time for equity investors. Then we witnessed the '87 crash, the dot.com bust, the '08 real estate/Lehmann crash and the Covid debacle, followed quickly by the inflation-fueled 2022 swoon. Surely even the most comatose buy-and-hold investor must intuit that performance could improve if only – if ONLY – s/he could avoid those bear markets, even if only partially.

When the Dow starts dropping, you have no idea how far "down" is really going to go. Maybe 800 points. Maybe 8000. When the 2008 real estate market threatened to crater the entire country, the Federal government flooded the banks with new money to lend out, coming to the market's rescue. Twelve years later there was no joy in Mudville until the Fed did a similar improv when the 2020 Covid Crash hit. The gummint outdid itself shoveling out money by the truckload – and inflation be damned. (They sang different tunes when the inevitable $6.00 gasoline signs went up, of course. (*Inflation? Oh, just 'transitory.'* My, how they do lie.) This "quick recovery" pattern has become so common that many investors came to expect it; they even RELY on it – and that's a mistake, Jake.

Expecting that next week must be similar to last week is called "recency bias" and it is always a fallacy. Psychologists tell us our brains are hard-wired to search for patterns – even when the patterns are merely illusions. If there's a full moon and you roll boxcars twice in a row, you have no rational reason to expect the third roll will also be two sixes. If you anticipate a three-peat is about to be rolled, that's pure recency bias; your brain spotting the start of a pattern that doesn't exist. Just because recent stock market drops were brief and have ended like valentines, doesn't mean the next one won't be an epic nightmare. By the early 2020s decade the

Federal Reserve rescued us out of enormous market drops, likely preventing far worse. But now we face alpha grizzlies like we haven't seen in young investors' lifetimes and to tame established patterns of price rises may require more economic faceboarding than congress or the general public will bear.

Nothing can serve you up an " aw-w-w, hell!" day like the S&P500.

----------------------.

MEMO from *The Stock Trader's Notebook:* A bull market is like sex. It feels best just before it ends.

-Barton Biggs

--------------------.

----------------------.

(Note: All the charts in this book are hand drawn sketches, simplified to clearly illustrate the principles. So sue me.)

Back To The Theory (just a bit more)

Let's agree for the moment that "ocean liner" stocks (if we can find some) are easier to predict than "flea" stocks.

Let's also agree, with all the many ways we can blunder into stock losses, that our emotions and opinions can be perverse tools in trading and investing. So what we might need is an objective method to track deep-volatility funds; a reliable and objective trigger telling us when to buy and when to sell, *without our having an opinion in the matter*. That trigger should be a dependable Technical Indicator which tracks our security and gives off an unmistakable trading signal. A good signal, if one exists, would instruct us to buy when it senses probability of a bullish trend ahead and likewise indicate when to sell as odds move against us. It would allow us to capture a portion (most or some) of most upcoming bullish trends and side-step probable downturns before the plunge could cause much loss.

Great. We know what we need, Snead. Now off to find it.

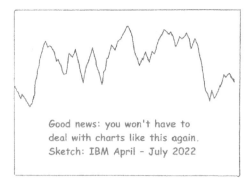

Good news: you won't have to deal with charts like this again.
Sketch: IBM April – July 2022

Our task: a discipline to throw hunches aside and focus exclusively on the deepest volatility assets we can find and apply technical indicators. Hence the name of our method is:

DVolT

I can't stress this enough, so get it in your head, Fred: the market doesn't care about your two university degrees, your GPA or your golf score. Your self confidence and bright, persuasive opinions, and all your other fine virtues are useless here. However convincing your arguments, however strong your certainty, we play by the market's rules, and Mr. Market does what Mr. Market wants, rational or not.

The market can be cruel as a mean-drunk thug. It devours bigger portfolios than yours or mine before 10 AM and doesn't glance back at the blood trail. Like the hairiest cracked-up biker, the market can defy all logic, reasoning and common-sense arithmetic, racing on a whim to extremes of highs or lows and doubling back when least expected. Just to be particularly cussed, the market might treat good economic news like a mugging and bad news like a lottery win. And your beliefs about all this? Mr. Market couldn't care less, Bess. I sometimes picture the market with a personality like the Greek god Zeus; petty, vengeful, selfish, violent, tricky, omnipotent but arbitrary. *(Wanna make Zeus laugh? Buy that penny stock.)*

On October 12, 2022 the new inflation numbers were the media's morning buzz. It seemed certain the Fed would raise interest rates another .75 of a point in November and probably again in December. Word from the latest Fed meeting was the gray-hairs were fretting that the risk of not raising rates enough was worse than raising them too much. So you had the prospect of a perfect bear storm that trading day. Sure enough, the DJIA gapped down

600 points at the open – and then promptly did the unbelievable; it touched bottom, rallied, and by the close of business had GAINED a net 800 points, an incredible 1400 point swing from low to high in a single day. Don't ever think you have the stock market figured out. You don't.

Still, if you're really shrewd, The Big Guy <u>can</u> be outwitted. You'll never handle Zeus with your suave manner; intelligent perspectives, insights, your dimples, your sparkling conversation, your cum laude degree, or anything, you regard as your worthiest qualities. When you come to outwit Zeus (come to beat the market) you'd better be a wise guy – shrewd and disciplined -- and carry a cattle prod for the bulls. Smart people who did well in school and who have been rewarded in their careers are accustomed to being right. They have confidence in their judgment and opinions – and that is why they often end up face down, chewing gravel. They're not wise guys. With this stock market, smarts ain't enough.

I don't lay this out to insult or depress you. I want to remind you where you stand in relation to the big fat bastard that is the New York Stock Exchange. It's our hard-earned savings we're about to invest. If a fool and his money are, you know, etc, etc, then you and I are going to tiptoe very carefully. OK?

OK, eggshells it is.

So here is the first answer to your *"Why isn't everyone doing it?"* zinger. Most investors simply cannot put their hunches and opinions aside. They can't, they won't! Where bloated egos fill crowded auditoriums and pot-fueled personas laugh at contrary news, what chance have wee little technical signals on a pathetic, forgotten chart? Almost all weak-kneed investors let their judgments and investment choices be tightly bound up in their outlooks, political leanings, and interpretations of news headlines. Never mind the difficulty of kicking the habit. They don't even realize they're doing it, and can't imagine working differently. And wouldn't if they could! Sure, they may study charts or read the news, but when new information contradicts earlier predictions or opinions, well, you know what they disregard, even if shown a more reliable technique.

When investing vanities die, they die hard. But you and I aren't going to try to impose our opinions on the market; we are going to flog the internal characteristics of a select few stocks and funds to our advantage.

The second reason "Why isn't everyone doing it?" is because few investors, (even those who try to follow technical indicators) have ever thought to marry chart discipline exclusively to the least volatile assets they can find. The DVolT method demands that you specialize; it requires that you greatly limit what stocks or funds you're willing to own. You can probably never buy Tesla, General Dynamics, Visa or Boeing. They are out. Apple, Cisco, Dycom? Fuggettaboutit, Fredo. How about Disney, Delta or Dell? Nope, uh-uh and no way. Not even Amazon? Quoth the raven: "Nevermore". They can't be considered. Get the drift? Those volatile stocks – and a thousand more – are taboo. Very few investors have ever thought of such drastic self-limitation or would be willing to practice the tactic if they did. Others come to the topic already certain that "market timing doesn't work". They seize upon any doubt to "prove" to themselves that their first opinion is the correct one. And from a certain viewpoint they're right. Technical analysis often won't work if you spread it around with a trowel on any hinky stocks that catch your fancy.

A third reason why people won't try to time the market is because they have tried and failed … they didn't know how to apply deep-volatility discipline … so suddenly the "no you can't" argument seems to look smart.

----------------.

MEMO from *The Stock Trader's Notebook:* **Once a cat has burned his butt, he won't even sit on a cold stove.**

----------------.

A fourth answer why DVolT isn't used: even if people thought of it; not many ever believed in it enough to do the grunt work of sifting through hundreds of trading assets to find those few with velvet-rolling chart histories. It's less work (and more fun in the dorm rooms) to just scoff than to make a long and diligent search.

But the good news is that I've already done search work for you. Stay with me here.

--------------------------.

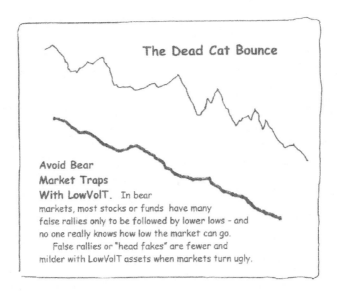

The Dead Cat Bounce

Avoid Bear
Market Traps
With LowVolT. In bear
markets, most stocks or funds have many
false rallies only to be followed by lower lows - and
no one really knows how low the market can go.
    False rallies or "head fakes" are fewer and
milder with LowVolT assets when markets turn ugly.

--------------------------.

MEMO from *The Stock Trader's Notebook:*

"Luck occurs when preparation meets opportunity." --Seneca

----------------.

So after decades of inhaling ink fumes from freshly printed Barron's, I finally found a side street to easy street -- a solution for a small investor might lie somewhere in disciplined trading of ultradeep volatility assets .... increasing allocations when trend lines (and probabilities!) curve favorably, and reducing when slopes begin to droop. In the end, I thought I wanted to invest like the ultimate wise guy – like Mr. Spock would on Starship Enterprise: making my decisions evidence-based, completely rational -- emotionless and opinion-free. And nothing complicated! We seek only the simplest information for our choices. We want data so elementary an imbecile couldn't misinterpret it. Like a Texas Hold'em player who lives or dies on his ability to smell the odds, we stay in the game only when probabilities are favorable. As a premise, I accept the fact that any opinion I develop today on a stock's future puts me at risk of falling into a "confirmation bias" attitude tomorrow. I'm in no way immune from bias – and neither are you. Once we finally understand our egos are our worst enemies – we vow to position ourselves with a Wise Guy's don't-give-a-damn attitude – about anything.

And who's your friend? The trend.... or to nail it down tighter, the <u>changes</u> in trend lines of deepest-volatility assets.

----------------------.

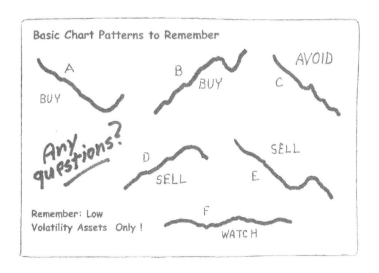

----------------.

But What About Diversification?

Over-rated. Effective diversification usually include stocks or funds best left to market snake-handlers; assets that move against the market like commodity funds sometimes do, or inverse (bearish) ETFs like SH or SDOW always do. Otherwise you're probably deluding yourself by "diversifying" among a lot of investments that are frequently correlated anyway. If twenty million gob-smacked investors needed to learn that lesson in 2008 and again in the 2020 market crashes, they should have learned it well. When markets face-plant, everything shreds. Stocks, gold, bonds, and even commodities may just as likely join the big wipeout as anything else. Your diversification avails you nothing precisely when you need it most. You can prove this to yourself by getting in the habit of making long term chart overlays and see how closely most stocks and funds actually move together in rough sympathy, especially in times of big market movements. When you find one that consistently zigs when others zag, that's a diversifying candidate. Good luck finding some.

Further, you're asking for trouble if you try to just buy and hold bearish protective funds in your portfolio. First of all, most are way too volatile to trade according to plan. But if you just *hold* a substantial amount of inverse funds for protection against a bear market, it will drag on your total portfolio's return like a half ton of lead whenever the market is bullish.

We'll get back to inverse funds and "going short" later. But for now, when I recall the mistakes I've made over the years and the success I had as I slowly gained tactical clarity and discipline, diversifying had nothing to do with it.

---------------------.

MEMO from *The Stock Trader's Notebook:*

Diversification is a protection against ignorance. It makes very little sense to those who know what they are doing. --Warren Buffett

---------------------.

Technical Trading Signals and You

Once you're settled on a couple of promising low volatility stocks or funds to trade, you need a reliable and objective trade trigger to signal – and no mistake – BUY NOW or SELL NOW.

Any professional pilot trainee learns a lesson in low visibility flying. In darkness or deep cloud cover, pilots learn to ignore their instincts and to trust the cockpit instruments. We all have confidence in our senses of balance and direction but the human body plays bizarre tricks on the pilot who makes decisions based on what s/he senses when flying blind.

Amateur investors find that putting opinions and hunches aside to "fly by the instruments" is hard to think about and tougher to actually do. But like any competent pilot, the DVolT investor must learn to "trust your gauges" and ignore your viewpoints. In your case, your instruments are going to be a few reliable technical indicators which we will add onto a simple, deep-volatility stock chart.

Wait and see -- deep volatility married to technical indicators is a thing of beauty and, working together, with your self discipline, they will benefit you enormously.

Say Hello To Your New (Second-Best) Friend --- The P-SAR

The next few paragraphs are going to be elementary for experienced traders, but stay with me here, guys. We'll get to you old-timers in a bit.

The Parabolic Stop and Reverse, or P-SAR is a generally reliable market timing indicator. It is free and available on Yahoo! Finance and other investment websites. It is objective. And you will see, when applied to a deep-volatility fund, it is accurate and useful.

But (again!) no technical indicator will work for you until you learn to ditch your emotions and your biases and to trade on cold, mathematical signals. Let's look at a rough sketch of Ford stock with the P-SAR.

Setting up P-SAR is simple..

1. Go to YAHOO CHARTS and plug in F (as a sample stock) If you see a candlestick chart, change it to a line chart.

2. Click on 1 Month

3. Scroll down "INDICATORS" and click on PSAR

Greatly simplified, you're going to see something like this:

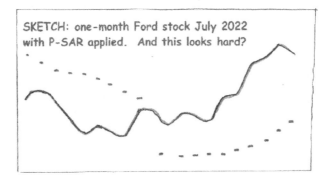

SKETCH: one-month Ford stock July 2022 with P-SAR applied. And this looks hard?

Those little dots you see are the P-SAR indicating bullish or bearish attitudes. So long as the dots are <u>underneath</u> the price line, that is your "bullish" signal (one dot for each day, or if you switch to one-week intervals on a longer term chart, one dot for each week). But so long as the dots are <u>above</u> the price line, that is your "avoid" signal. You can see our sample chart sketch starts out bearish, but on the tenth day you see the dot pattern hops from above the price line to below it. That is your BUY signal. You buy immediately and remain holding Ford until the dots hop back above the line and you promptly sell.

Let's think this out a bit.

Root Canal, Selling Stocks, and Other Fun Stuff

Does this ring a bell? *"OMG! Just <u>look</u> at that sick bitch. I'm a genius! It's WAY up. HOT damn! But I can't lose those gains. It'll kill me if I do. I hear gold is up but wheat is down. United Widgits had a bad quarter. CNN predicts rain in Spain. Putin has the sniffles. Does that spell trouble? Should I sell and keep my gains? But what if it keeps going up? Should I sell??*

Or how about --- *"OMG! Last week that dumb-ass stock was up and now it's crashed! Why didn't I sell that stupid cur when I had the gains? Should I sell now? But what if it rallies tomorrow? Cramer says BUY, but my old man says SELL. Maybe I should wait – but it could drop even more. I KNEW I shouldn't have bought that POS. SHOULD I SELL?"*

That old Wall Street saying: "Sell your losers and let your winners run" is as valid today as it was a century ago. Your P-SAR indicator is your first tool to work that rule. Remember we seek to avoid either over-confidence or its twin, paralyzing fear. We reject both cockiness and jitters by flying with our P-SAR cockpit instrument. If you're an active trader who rather enjoys checking his portfolio frequently, you'll set up your chart's P-SAR so it gives you a signal every trading day. But if you have a real life and little time for fretting in front of a computer monitor, Yahoo! Finance lets genuine long-term investors set up their chart so the P-SAR throws out a signal only weekly. (When setting up your Yahoo! Chart, just change the INTERVAL box from 1D to 1W). Either set-up is valid, so long as you remain consistent and disciplined. (Actually, I prefer the daily signal over the weekly. If a stock I own is starting to break down, I don't want to wait a week to find out about it. But hey, that's me, McFee.)

--------------.

I spent half my money on gambling, alcohol and wild women. The other half I wasted.

------------------.

Selling Problems: Solved. From now on you never need to anguish over when to sell because *you are going to hold any position so long as your chosen indicator remains in "bullish" mode*. Whether it's six days or six months, you're not going to touch that DVolT stock – you won't even think about unloading– until that P-SAR flips. No more doubts or second-guessing yourself. Understand you already made your "sell" decision the moment you bought your Ford stock: when your chart indicators change, you act. Period.

Your determination to heed your signals and hold any position so long as it continues trending upward will be a powerful protection from falling prey to the **disposition effect,** one of the worst habits of poor investors who tend to sell assets that are increasing in value, while clinging to stocks that have dropped in value because they are desperate to be right and reluctant to admit they were wrong.

Key to DVolT thinking is you must learn to act without delay, without anxiety or emotions. You are putting aside your hunches and replacing them with consistency and cold-hearted objectivity. This may be a novel idea for you, to ignore your judgments and hunches, but if you're squirming about now, what can I say? Remember we talked in the opening pages how wedded you were to your habits and opinions.

Recall also we agreed that "ocean liner" stocks were more predictable than "flea" stocks, so if we are consistent, we must remind ourselves (again and again if necessary!) when a DVolT stock changes direction it has a decent probability of continuing in that new direction.

OK then, let's put it together. I'm asking you to limit yourself to the most predictable trading assets we can find and, like a good poker player, learn to *play the probabilities*. Over any short time period, the typical one-day probability of a stock going up overnight is about 50/50. With DVolT the probability may be about 55/45. So the day after you buy your first DVolT asset you really can't be confident that stock or fund is about to go up the next few hours. But you have good reason to believe the probabilities are in your favor over the next few days because it has begun *trending* upward – and in the past that particular stock has tended to maintain trend changes. Your indicator doesn't predict what will happen as the minutes tick by, but it has a fairly high accuracy of predicting DVolT stocks over the course of a few days or a few weeks. The skilled DVolT investor assumes a wise guy's devil-may-care attitude. S/he doesn't much care what happens the second or third days after buying a new position because, over the course of many buys and sells, when you're wrong your losses will usually be quick and small but when you are right your gains will usually be much larger. When you make wrong choices, the P-SAR indicator you applied to your deep-volatility fund will show the market moving against you, and you will be able to exit quickly with only a small loss. With your chart and your signals simple and clear, you can act promptly. Over time, your losses will be shallower than your gains.

And you will succeed.

"What to do when the market goes down? Read the opinions of the investment gurus who are quoted in the Wall Street Journal. And, as you read, laugh. We all know that the pundits can't predict short-term market movements. Yet there they are, desperately trying to sound intelligent when they really haven't got a clue."

-Jonathan Clements

-----------------.

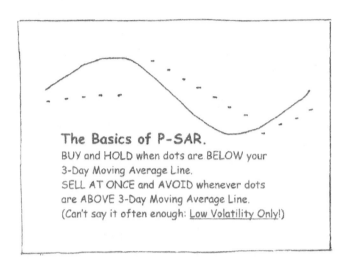

The Basics of P-SAR.
BUY and HOLD when dots are BELOW your
3-Day Moving Average Line.
SELL AT ONCE and AVOID whenever dots
are ABOVE 3-Day Moving Average Line.
(Can't say it often enough: Low Volatility Only!)

-----------------.

MEMO from The *Stock Trader's Notebook:* "It's not whether you're right or wrong that's important, but how much money you make when you're right and how much you lose when you're wrong." — George Soros

--------------------.

Risk: Hold That Tiger!

Well of course every new investment is a risk. There is always risk, but your disciplined DVolT practices are going to help keep it on a leash. Again and again, we pound the table: deep-volatility assets (with their histories of gently rolling climbs and dips) tend to change slowly enough for you to exit before serious damage is done. I want you to participate when your asset is climbing – but to side-step the worst of market plunges. It drives me crazy when I hear an investor remark, "Oh, I am going to stay the course" when market trends turn ugly. What "stay the course" or "buy-and-hold" mean is that you are determined to passively accept whatever losses the market slams you with – even when you know the probabilities are against you! You are going to stand outside and face the hurricane when you might just as easily step indoors and bolt the door. You're at a blackjack table holding 17; the stone-faced dealer shows a 3 and you say "Hit me."

Illogical? Yes, but millions of investors do it because "stay the course" has generally worked in the overall bull markets of recent years. They don't know any better – or if they know better, they're irrationally stubborn. They do it because they believe the old claim "you can't time the market".

Oh yes you can, Fran.

---------------------------.

MEMO from *The Stock Trader's Notebook:* "Though tempting, trying to time the market is a loser's game. $10,000 continuously invested in the market over the past 20 years grew

to more than $48,000. If you missed just the best 30 days, your investment was reduced to $9,900." --*Christopher Davis*

Very interesting, but what would the total return be if you missed only ten of the best 30 days while missing 50 of the 100 WORST days? Mr. Davis doesn't say. DVolT traders specialize in avoiding those bear trends.

-------------------------.

Other folks who think of themselves as long term investors stay invested in all markets because that's what the big broker advertisements have advised their customers to do. "Don't try to time the market! Stay the course and you'll do well," has been the mantra that mullahs of marketing have lectured the public since the 1950s right up until today. The advertisers get away with such advice because A) we have lived through such an extraordinary period of gains so B) many investors could not even remember what a true bear market looks or feels like until 2008 began its crumbling process. But step inside the trading floors of the big investment houses and you'll see at once that practically none of them have a "stay the course" philosophy for their own money. Do you really think hedge fund bond traders work a "buy and hold" strategy in all kinds of markets? Are their quants and AI computer trading programs geared up to ride it out over the long term?

LOL, as the kids would say.

Certainly the super rich can afford to park their massive wealth in a diversified portfolio of luxe real estate and blue chip stocks and give nary a thought to market trends. They can pack up their krugerrands in gallon zip-lock bags and wheel them down to the local Wells Fargo vault's big box. An eight thousand point crash in the DJIA would have precisely zero effect on the lifestyles of Bill Gates, Kevin Costner or quarterback Tom Brady. But for the likes of you or me, staying pat in a grinding bear market and seeing your retirement nest egg or your kid's college savings hemorrhage away week by week --- and doing nothing – is that intelligent management? Well, imagine it. The market is steadily dropping and at a certain point your worry turns to a feeling of shame; you begin to have glum thoughts of having missed a great opportunity. "How," you ask, "could I have been so stupid?" as the market continues grinding downward. When all the predictions are direst, when somber voices drone the litany of economic woes on television, when we all realize that this time it truly IS different – that the Fed will NOT be coming to our rescue as we are accustomed to – well, you know chances are excellent you too will cave, perhaps near the worst possible moment. It's human nature. Despite all your previous intentions when the bull market was romping, you will sell.

Wall Street wise guys love that moment so much they have a special word for it: *capitulation*, the hour when the last of the little people surrender in hope of rescuing their remaining shreds of wealth, driving stock prices down to their lowest. (They use "capitulation" because it sounds better than "kick 'em in the nuts".) That's the moment shrewd traders sitting on boatloads of cash love because they sold profitably near the top – that's the moment they begin to buy at bargain prices. Shortly after the miserable suckers have sold out, the beaten-down market at last begins to climb, and the grand old cycle repeats again, as it always has since the trading of equities began.

----------.

He's your guy

When stocks are high,

But beware when they start to descend.

It's then that those louses

Go back to their spouses.

Diamonds are a girl's best friend!

--from "Gentlemen Prefer Blondes"

------------.

Although all bear markets are different, they often share similar characteristics. Younger investors, full of piss and vinegar, never imagine such a scenario. They weren't even born when the last extended bear market beginning in the early 1970s ground hopes and portfolios to dust. They were just children in 2008 and by 2020 no true extended bear market had ever occurred in their time frames. As for those older long-term investors and savers who were invested during the plug ugly 2007 – 2008 scares, subsequent recoveries tend to efface their recollections. "It turned all right in the end, so why should I worry today?" they might remark with memories fading. Bull markets do have a way of causing bitter lessons to be forgotten.... until a new terrible bear market roars, and millions of forgetful investors are trapped yet again. When the S&P500 drops, say, below 20%, confidence in a quick bounce-back begins to slip to worry and then to anguish. Headlines turn universally dour. Earning reports come out and no numbers seem good enough. Mr. Market, sadist that he is, lifts hopes with a rally or two, only to crash even lower than before. By now the smart money has long since fled to cash, watching from the sidelines, half in glee, half anxious not to miss the bottom.

The retail investors sell in ever-larger numbers. Eyes turn anxiously to the Fed. Will it save us from our fate as it has regularly done before or is it actually encouraging the drop by tightening credit and hiking interest rates? Eventually, if no savior appears, panic may be at hand. Those who have never seen a collapsing market, who cannot imagine a "no bottom" crash are ill prepared for the ugly trend that will come – as come it will. But DVolT investors will have planned their tactics long before the black event looms. They will survive and even thrive.

Overall, it is very true that buy-and-hold has served small investors well over recent decades. But we're looking forward from the mid 2020s now. This is the stock market of short memories. Many barely recollect despair and real fear.

-----------------------.

MEMO from *The Stock Trader's Notebook:*

One book every investor should try to find is Sy Harding's "RIDING THE BEAR". The first fifty pages or so are some of the most important chapters ever written for the small investor. Harding lays his case out in compelling style – that normally, over-bought markets and bear markets usually work in natural rhythms. Since you can be dead-cinch sure another bear market lurks in your future, the wise guy investor thinks of the market as working in repeating cycles, not in a near-eternal trend.

As good as its first chapters are, Riding The Bear, published 1989, is undeniably dated as later chapters address the 1990s market, and Harding is never quite able to come up with a really effective timing protocol. In the end, he more or less falls back on variations of the old "Sell in May and go away..." mantra. While he lays out numbers to show that holding stocks in winter and spring while selling summers and autumns does frequently work very well, his thinking doesn't allow for the flexibility DVolT offers.

Followers of Harding would have been slaughtered in the Covid Crash of 2020, but DVolT traders dodged the worst of the bullet.

-----------------------.

Candlestick vs Area Charts (Or "Mountain" Charts). What's the deal, O'Neal?

In everything we do, we aim for simplicity and clarity. The essentials are the only information we want. We're not day traders and for us, the candlestick charts throw off too many irrelevant details. Of course I understand many traders are comfortable using candlestick charts; there is no compelling need for them to change. Nevertheless for simplicity and clarity, I opt for area charts (or "mountain" charts) every time.

Your 'Trade-Confirmation' Trigger

I'll remind you again: back on the early pages we asked if you were determined to be a successful trader and would you, could you, change an old habit? Might you really re-consider your viewpoint?

Well, here's your test, Celeste. I'm going to ask you to set up your Yahoo! chart in a way you've never done before. Here we go....

(You investing veterans might think to skip this next part..... but don't! As you'll see in a page or two, it becomes critical for you also!)

Even the quiet ETFs (exchange traded funds) sometimes show too much "noise" in their charts for confident trading. The emotional effect of money on the line with sharp little "V's" in a chart often confuses us and prompts us to take action where none is warranted. The technique I'm about to describe reduces one cause of poor choices by making a lower volatility chart mimic a deep-volatility pattern.... as long as you don't abuse it.

You don't need sophisticated software. We're returning to good ol' yahoo.com for our tool development. Young investors can be forgiven if they take Yahoo! charts for granted; the online service has been around all their lives. But older investors know there was a time when the notion having free tools for adjusting charts and indicators for different views and values was unheard of.

OK, here we go. This is important. Test yourself with the following steps to set up a trading chart for Berkshire Hathaway "B". It may seem strange, but bear with me – just follow along step by step .

Go to Yahoo.com / finance.

Enter BRK-B and hit "CHART"

A large chart of BRK-B comes up. If you see CANDLE, change it to LINE. You will see something like this:

------------------------.

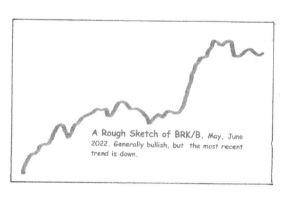

A Rough Sketch of BRK/B. May, June 2022. Generally bullish, but the most recent trend is down.

--------------------.

Now, click on 1M for your short term One Month time frame

Under INDICATORS, scroll down and click on MOVING AVERAGES. Where it says "50" I want you to change it to 3. (Yes,

I said 3. Not a misprint.)

_____.

MEMO for beginners: *A "three-day moving average" tracks the average price of the previous three days. It is much smoother than the actual minute-by-minute price line.*

A 15-Day Moving Average will be the average price of the previous 15 days. It will obviously be much calmer than even the 3-Day MA.

In stock market lingo, we'd refer to the 3-Day Moving Average as the "fast line" and the 15-Day Moving Average as the "slow line". Got that?

------------.

Return to INDICATORS again and click on MOVING AVERAGES a second time. Where it says "50", change it to 15, but make sure your two moving average lines are different colors. You now have something like this:

-----------------.

A Similar Sketch
But this time we add a 3-Day Moving Average and a 15-Day Moving Average.

———— 3-Day MA —●—●—●— 15-Day MA

------------------.

Important: before we move on I want you to take a moment and carefully observe how closely the 3-Day Moving Average line tracks the true price line. To put it in other words, the two lines never stray far apart. Also notice those few instances when the actual price line moves more forcefully, creating a sharp little peak or knife-edge dip. You will see, immediately after, the two lines inevitably tend to jerk right back closer to each other. When there is line separation, it doesn't last for long. See that? Good.

Now here's where it gets fun. In the upper left of your chart you will see three little boxes: BRK-B, MA-3 and MA-15. Now trust me here -- click on the little BRK-B box and then click on the little colored box that appears. You will see a range of colors. *I want you to select the faintest, whitest shade you can find. I want you to make your BRK-B price line practically INVISIBLE. The fainter, the better. Don't yell, Nell. Just do it.*

Now return to the big chart you've set up and here's what you have:

A 3-Day Moving Average Price Line

A 15-Day Moving Average Price Line

A true price line for BRK-B, (but you can't see it!)

Your price line is practically gone. But you have your manageable, smooth three-day and fifteen-day moving averages to guide you. Since you already know BRK-B rarely makes violent, sudden moves, you can be confident the 3-Day MA is tracking it quite closely, just as you noticed earlier. Also, if you decide to add P-SAR, it will still magically track the actual price line you can no longer see. (Hereafter you work like a physician using x-rays. You can't see the actual bone, but you can make effective decisions based on the shadows that remain visible.)

-------------.

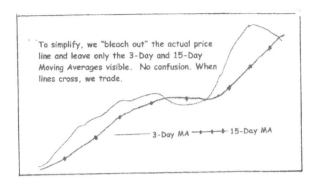

To simplify, we "bleach out" the actual price line and leave only the 3-Day and 15-Day Moving Averages visible. No confusion. When lines cross, we trade.

——— 3-Day MA ⊶⊶⊶ 15-Day MA

Almost all the distracting "chart noise" has vanished. The almost meaningless pops and drops are erased. What remains are highly effective trading signals. If you have added P-SAR for an additional signal system on the same chart you might use it as your initial BUY signal when it occurs and your 3 x 15 "CROSSOVER" point (where the 3-day MA crosses over the 15-day MA) as your confirmation to add more stock to make a bigger position Again, you make a small buy when you get the first signal (the P-SAR) and a larger buy when/if you see confirmation (the moving average crossover), or vice versa.

If the P-SAR trips more often than you like, ordering you to trade more frequently than you wish, you can dispense with it altogether. For fewer trades and fewer signals, you can ditch the P-SAR and just use your 3 x 15-day crossovers as your only buy/sell signals. So long as you apply only Deep Volatility stocks and funds, you will do well. Hour-by-hour price exactitude avails you very little if a close approximation helps you make better trades.

However close the 3-day moving average hugs the true (and now invisible!) deep volatility stock or fund price line, you can make it even closer if you opt for the 2-Day Moving Average instead of the 3-Day. In either case what is now greatly reduced are the sharp "zig-zags," the price-flutters and little head-fakes that can cause you paralysis in making good decisions. Deploying the 2-day or 3-day MA instead of the true price line is an intelligent compromise to use with almost any deep-volatility stock or fund. We are swapping hour-by-hour accuracy for a clearer trend picture to make better choices. The two-day or three-day line is an approximation of the reality.... and with DVolT almost always a close approximation.

----------------------.

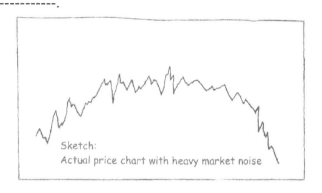

Sketch:
Actual price chart with heavy market noise

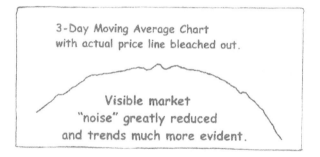

3-Day Moving Average Chart
with actual price line bleached out.

Visible market
"noise" greatly reduced
and trends much more evident.

----------------------.

OBJECTION! *If I trade on the 3-Day Moving Average, the chart I see will always be a little inaccurate. More importantly, if there is a sudden market crash or a spike in price, the extent of the sudden change will not fully show upon my tweaked chart until later.*

Response: Well of course. That's the reason why we use deep volatility trading assets in the first place; to minimize most unusually big, sudden price changes. Let's step back and think about what we know.

A. We are sure that even a low-volatility stock has little jumps and dips which are actually immaterial to its broader trend, correct?

B. We have also seen that the 2-day or 3-day moving average line closely hugs the true price line of the low-volatility stock, true?

If "A" and "B" are both correct, then the true price line of our deep volatility chart becomes a distracting complication! The chart with two different moving averages AND the true price line simply throws off too much information – much of it distracting. But in removing the true price line, you give your emotions or hunches less subjective room to see what you want to see. By keeping only what is truly important, you have less reason to fret or delay when critical information appears.

Let's take another look at the "bleach-out benefit" in the three charts below, this time with GE stock. Even with a greatly simplified sketch, the top chart has many little back-and forth movements, any one of which might prod you into making a foolish, emotional move. Remember, where ever you are, you have only a guess of what is about to happen next. All your doubts and emotions are in full play as news headlines blast at you while the price line zigs and zags day by day.

Then the middle chart throws more worrisome details at you. But everything becomes clear and obvious in the bottom chart. Your emotions have far less opportunity to push you if minor distractions are removed and you simply watch for the crossovers. Notice (after a brief head-fake at the start that costs you little or nothing) how much you saved by selling promptly (when the 3-DMA crossed under the 15-DMA) and avoiding the big drop that followed. Then see how much you gained by buying promptly and holding when the 3-DMA line crossed back over the15-DMA and you *held without worry* so long as your moving averages remained bullish.

This is DVolT at work.

-----------------------.

Another Look —

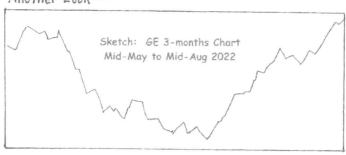

Sketch: GE 3-months Chart
Mid-May to Mid-Aug 2022

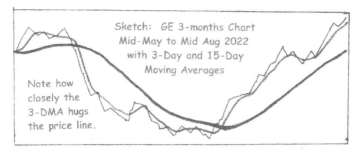

Sketch: GE 3-months Chart
Mid-May to Mid Aug 2022
with 3-Day and 15-Day
Moving Averages

Note how
closely the
3-DMA hugs
the price line.

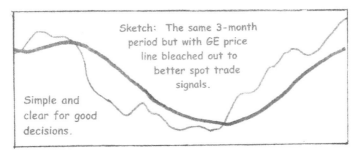

Sketch: The same 3-month
period but with GE price
line bleached out to
better spot trade
signals.

Simple and
clear for good
decisions.

-----------------------.

Here the veteran investor might laugh and snort with indignation. *"This is insulting and ridiculous! I'm perfectly capable of watching three little lines simultaneously. You don't have to dumb down your stupid charts for me to make MY choices."*

I reply, "Are you sure? When markets are flowing, time is ticking by, news headlines blaring, and your nerves feel the stress of money of the table – do you really feel you're the one-in-a-million whose choices don't improve when information becomes clearer?" In the opening pages of this book I stressed that clarity is essential. I repeat: the truth is WE DON'T KNOW how our mental distractions or unknown inclinations work under the stresses of time passing with dollars at risk and uncertainty ahead. I believe we all can make better choices – more CONFIDENT decisions -- when information is honed down to essentials.

This is a "look into yourself moment" for any reader who disdains a simpler chart when it is offered to him. I would suggest you'd be displaying exactly the kind of stubborn and irrational rigidity we discussed in our opening pages. And let's consider the true-life realities. At that moment, as you're sitting there, considering the chart, is that truly the only thing you're concerned with? Let's imagine something like the truth: your car's motor oil needs to be changed before your trip Thursday, the kids are fussing in the next room, you're annoyed your spouse has been doubting your investment choices recently, the kitchen window won't latch shut, another orthodontist bill just landed on your desk, the neighbor's dog is yapping again and you have ten more stock charts to look at after this one. Are you really sure distractions and unseen biases aren't hovering around?

Our goal is consistently shrewd choices. Simplicity is one of our tools.

Like on old-time radio, *"Yes, folks. In moments of stress and uncertainty, always reach for that handy bottle of Old Clarity in your medicine cabinet. Relief is just moments away."*

AN ALTERNATIVE

When it comes to technical indicators, truly a "less is more" situation develops. More indicators mean more information thrown at you and one can easily slip into "signal paralysis" or information overload. Add one indicator too many and timely decisions become more difficult. So I hope even skilled investors won't use more than two technical indicators on their charts. One is better, IMO, and many times I have worked successfully that way. But the P-SAR and moving averages aren't the only technical indicators. There are others you should know about.

Once you become comfortable using P-SAR or your two moving averages applied to DVolT, you might consider trying the STOCHASTIC MOMENTUM INDICATOR as presented on Yahoo!

It's easily done on your existing Yahoo! chart like you've done before: Scroll down under INDICATORS and click on STOCHASTIC MOMENTUM INDEX (SMI) . And you're done. (If you prefer, on a Three-Month chart, use the 2-day Moving Average as an option instead of the 3-Day. 3-Day MA is just too slow to use on a one-month chart.) But for a One Year chart, I like keeping the 3-day moving average line as my smoothing proxy. Bleach out the true price line. And, if you wish, you can even retain your 15-Day Moving Average. Just don't get yourself lured in by too many indicators!

With the SMI in the mix, you have some real techno-sophistication working in your corner, and it is just wonderful to use in harness with DVolT stocks. They complement each other well. On Yahoo! charts the SMI consists of a red line and a black line crossing back and forth over and under each other. When people talk about the SMI, they often focus on the "overbought/oversold" signals. But those are two aspects of SMI that don't much interest me. What I find useful is its "divergence/convergence" action. When the lines move to increase their separation, momentum is strengthening, but when the two lines trend ever-closer to one another, the trend is weakening.

Their actual cross is your buy/sell trigger. But here's the beautiful part; if you look closely, you see the SMI senses an increase or decrease in momentum BEFORE the actual cross-over occurs. It can give a fairly reliable early warning that the momentum is becoming stronger or weaker a couple of days before your trade signal actually crosses! With experience, you will appreciate how SMI often telegraphs the momentum lagging or gaining steam even before the price has moved strongly, giving you an early warning of trends to come.

There is another advantage SMI has over P-SAR. If a stock or fund has had a sudden big move, your P-SAR can be temporarily thrown out of whack for several days. In 2022 Netflix surprised the market with an announcement it had been losing subscribers for the first time in its history. NFLX crashed over 30% the next trading day. For days thereafter its P-SAR remained locked on "sell" signals no matter what NFLX stock did. Or you may find an ETF or closed end fund announces a special end-of-year dividend. When that happens the stock or fund price suddenly drops in anticipation of big money leaving the fund and into accounts. You, the investor, won't feel any pain because you are receiving a large cash distribution to compensate for the sudden plunge in share price, but the P-SAR may be unreliable for a week or more. It will most likely remain at a "sell" signal even while the fund is clearly recovering from its sudden price drop. Here's where SMI seems to be a better signal. In my experience it generally seems to recover from a sudden event more quickly and dependably.

But don't lose track of P-SAR's big advantage: it is as clear as an ON/OFF switch. It leaves no room for interpretation. I found through experience that my biases and emotions still have a way of slipping into my decisions even when I am determined to be disciplined. P-SAR gives you no wiggle-room. It's as unmistakable as a slap on the face – just GET IN or GET OUT!

You also have the very popular **Moving Average Convergence Divergence (MACD)** indicator which follows trends and momentum as an alternative to your P-SAR or SMI. Since the MACD gives indications when a momentum is strengthening or weakening, many investors prefer it as their primary signal, but it lacks the P-SAR's clear and distinct trading message. You will be well served if you turn to the MACD, but be aware you may need to put a bit of judgment or opinion into your trading – something I remain suspicious of.

-------------------.

MEMO from *The Stock Trader's Notebook:* "A plan is only useful if it can survive reality and a future filled with unknowns is everyone's reality. In the past century the stock market fell more than 10% from a recent high at least 102 times. Stocks lost a third of their value at least 12 times." (From THE PSYCHOLOGY OF MONEY – Morgan Housel)

-------------------.

When To Disregard The P-SAR

You will remember we discussed using the 3 x 15-day Moving Average crossover as either your first or your confirming "BUY" signal which you should see before you ever buy a large position. Well enough. But you should never buy any big position when your 15-day MA is still in a downward slope and your 3-day MA is underneath it! You've heard it. You know it. Still it bears repeating – don't touch that falling knife.

If you refuse to buy when you see those downward slopes, no matter what your P-SAR signals, you will save yourself some serious coin.

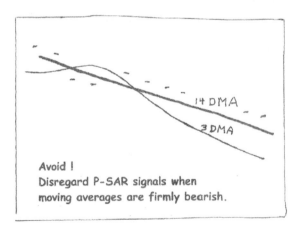

Avoid !
Disregard P-SAR signals when moving averages are firmly bearish.

And that is why we call P-SAR our "second best" friend. **Your two moving averages, with their slopes and their crossovers, should almost always take precedence in decision-making.**

And again, another problem many people have with the P-SAR is that it tends to encourage too much trading. If you are one of those who are uncomfortable making frequent trades, you'll do better to delete the P-SAR signal from your Yahoo! charts and use moving averages cross-overs as the only signal you really need in D-VolT investing.

As we discussed earlier, you can also cure the problem by extending your interval from 1D to 1W. You'll get far fewer trading signals – but just remember you're adding some risk if you invest ordinary volatile stocks on 1-week interval charts.

Head Fakes, Whiplash and Hiccups

It's fate. It can't be helped. No matter how carefully you invest you will experience "whiplash" or "head-fake" moves created as a stock rises, triggers a bullish signal, and then slips right back down again a couple of days later. Even with DVolT assets, these fast-changing signals can frustrate you no end as you move in and out of positions more often than you want to. No avoiding it. One of these days a curvaceous chart will sashay before you, promising a big wet kiss, but holding a brick behind her back. Heartbreakers are part of the game, like myopic baseball umpires or daydreaming football referees. You will probably lose money on such quick "round trips", but your losses will actually tend to be quite small compared to your big gains. So be consoled. Notice how much you do make when you get a "buy" signal that stretches out for weeks. Equally important -- see how much you avoid losing if you are disciplined enough to sell promptly whenever a signal tells you to. But it's a mistake trying to fit a square HiVolT stock into a round DVolT hole. Don't do it.

And look on the bright side; you're not limiting yourself – you're concentrating.

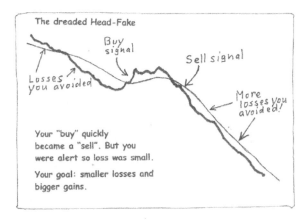

The dreaded Head-Fake

Buy signal

Sell signal

Losses you avoided

More losses you avoided!

Your "buy" quickly became a "sell". But you were alert so loss was small.

Your goal: smaller losses and bigger gains.

Let's make another general rule: the avoidance of loss should take precedence over achieving gains. Say Mr. Jones has a $10,000 portfolio and gains 50%, bringing him up to $15,000. Once there, he'd have to lose 33% to be back to $10,000. Elementary. So what? Now say Mr. Arnold also has a $10,000 portfolio and he (poor sap) loses 50%. He's down to $5000, but now he has to claw back a full 100% to return to his original $10k. While it is possible to recover from serious loss, it is harder to do than climbing from success to higher success. In my experience, equities can often collapse downward harder and faster than they generally climb. We all know of frightening historic dates when markets crashed, but there has never been a violent bullish explosion in a day or even in a week. Even worse, bear markets often appear far more volatile than upward trends. If that observation is valid, then my protective sell triggers should be more sensitive than my buy triggers. If you agree that downdrafts may be more violent than bull markets, we can consider the wisdom of selling more aggressively than we buy when confronted with new signals. That is why I'm suggesting it should take two buy signals to accumulate into any major position but only one sell signal to get mostly out. When it comes to euphoria melting, markets plunging and fearful bear market headlines, wise guys never ask "if". They want to know A) how deep? B) for how long? And, of course C) when?

Always protect what you had, Tad.

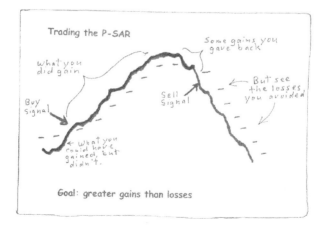

--------------------.

DVolT fits right into this notion of minimizing risk. Its beauty in preserving wealth for those instances when you are wrong is that you limit yourself to only a few low-volatility funds and your quick SELL/BUY whiplashes will be fewer in number and, more importantly, you lose very little in the process. It is impossible to tell if a new "sell" signal will be quickly reversed or if it is the start of a big bear trend. So: (yes, again!) swallow your hunches and follow the signal.

--------------------.

Three-Line Plan   PSF   Oct 1 – Dec 30, 2022

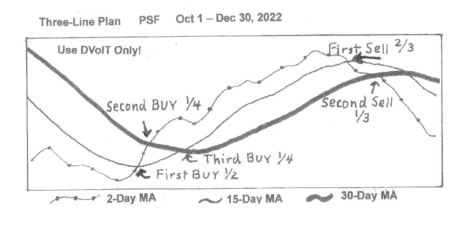

MEMO from *The Stock Trader's Notebook:*

Use of 3-line tactical moving averages alone. Acquire a stock or fund on confirming bullish signals but control somewhat more aggressive sales on bearish reversals.

--------------------.

A Caution for the Faint-Hearted

In real-world trading you will have no shortage of moments to fail D-VolT if you lose concentration or self discipline. While screwing up is easy, the actual reasons for D-VolT failure are few. One of the simplest and most common face-plants is to hesitate when a clear signal appears. Whether from self doubt or from lack of attention, you may find yourself with a real conumdrum if you let several days pass without acting on a clear signal. Remember your work is based on the probability of trends, not on their certainty. If you have trimmed your assets down to a few deep-volatility candidates, and have also stripped your charts down to lean-and-mean essentials, any new change in trends you see are apt to continue.

Say you get a P-SAR "BUY" signal on MMT and, for one reason or another, you do nothing. Three days later MMT is still trending up and you get your confirming moving average cross-over "buy" signal, but you wait to make sure. REAL sure. The following week MMT is up again and now you hesitate because so much of your potential profits have already passed you by. Or imagine that the very morning you finally make up your mind to make a purchase, MMT slips a little, so you decide to wait a bit to see if it slips more.

Talking yourself out of a DVolT trade is seductively easy – and usually a mistake. We have already built a loss-limiting trigger into your D-VolT discipline, so your probable gains are almost always bigger than your probable losses. Your failures increase with inattention if you don't act with prompt discipline.

Finally – Exactly <u>What</u> to Trade?

We've discussed DVolT funds and stocks, but which exactly are they and where can they be found? One of the established means to determine low volatility stocks and funds is to measure the standard deviations of price movements. That measurement is all well and good, but it's not very helpful in determining what assets you want to trade. Monthly standard deviation outliers say very little on the information we really need to know; not so much how far the outlier movements extend, but how sharply prices move up or down. Textbook measurements mostly determine the magnitude of outlying leaps and plunges stocks have moved but give us less information on their frequency. For our trading purposes, a stock that plunges downward 30% over the course of one trading day is much worse than the stock that takes three days to make the same move. Go through a list of equities labeled "low volatility stocks" and you'll see plenty of them juking and head-faking like most any others, only perhaps their peaks and pits won't be quite so high or deep as other typical securities on your list. That is why technical analysis isn't very effective for stocks commonly described as "low volatility" nor for most of the so-called "Low Volatility" ETFs that hold those stocks like USMV, SPLV or FDLO.

For DVolT searching purposes I haven't found anything to replace the grunt work of going through lists of stocks and likely ETFs and closed end funds (CEFs). I enter them on a three-month chart and simply count how many P-SAR reversals I see, disregarding any one-day back-and-forth signals. The fewer reversals the better. It's hardly a consistent method. Just because I count only five reversals for April-May-June doesn't mean there won't be eight or nine during July-August-September, but it does create a good tentative list for beginning work.

After many searches I've found there aren't very many really good DVolT candidates for us, and I'm never satisfied with the list I have. A stock may be trending quietly and tamely for a year or more but hit a violent patch when some CFO absconds to Brazil with his mistress and $80 million in cash. At other times a stock may be hopping about in normal volatility but just quiets down for some unknown reason. (Don't trust those!) Things happen, you know, and I don't think any DVolT list will ever be permanent. But some stocks and funds do come up repeatedly on almost any ultra-low volatility list.

At the time of publication, in no particular order, I'm listing the funds and stocks I currently like to use for my DVolT trading. I have separated them into two groups; the best securities to trade and the "B List".

Best: AOM, MMT, YYY, BGX, PGP, BOND, DFP, FPE, TOTL, TLT/TBF, SRLN, VFMV

B List: SPE, BRK/B, MUA, DSL, FTF, HNDL, HYB, SDIV, WIW, SPYD, FUND

That's it ? !

That's it.

At first blush, you might be dismayed by how short the lists are until you reflect that by limiting yourself to a "DVolT25" give or take a couple, you'll be able to watch those assets very closely. You're no longer scattering your attention over every new headline and news report blasting from your TV. You don't have to think of yourself as being constrained. You are specializing. You don't need a lot of stock choices to be successful. You just need a lot of wins, and bigger wins than losses.

And yes, less really can be more. With a little thought, you might see you're positioning yourself with terrific advantage if your portfolio consists of only five, six or seven investments. Consider the inevitable. Sooner or later the market is going to head south again, and when it does, picture yourself widely dispersed with twenty different positions. Your technical signals start flashing "Sell!" all over the place (but the news headlines typically say "Don't Panic") so you probably unload three, maybe four big positions and feel you've done a good day's work, but you're still long sixteen or seventeen more positions in a falling market. Maybe the next day you dawdle because the market seems to be firming a bit, but those signals are still bearish. The third day you sell two or three more positions, but all this time while you're stretching out the selling process, your portfolio is leaking money. It may take you a week (or even two!) to really respond to a important bear-market reversal and rid yourself of weak positions. This has really happened to me just as I'm describing it. (And more than once, I blush to confess.) When the market starts drifting down, nothing serious but clearly bearish, no one feels any terror, but your signals are popping. When that day comes, how likely are you to leap into some mini-selling marathon and dump ten big positions in one afternoon? Aren't you more likely to sell one or two and "see what happens"? And that will be how you might fail your D-VolT discipline, even with the best of intentions.

But if you voluntarily limit yourself to just four or five big positions, you're enjoying exposure to any bull market, but always optimally prepared to respond expeditiously to a reversal. You're like a well-run firehouse; your guys may be sitting around playing cards, but all the gear is pre-placed and pre-planned to quickly rumble whenever the alarm sounds. And don't forget if you own an equity exchange traded fund (ETF) or closed end fund (CEF) you're probably already exposed to dozens of stocks that fund is holding. I'll say it again; wide diversification is over-rated and simplicity under-appreciated. Always be ready, Freddy.

Of all the good DVolT candidates, a few have been most dependable, but every time I do another search for promising stocks and funds I can never come up with the same list twice. Whenever I collect a dozen good candidates I always find a thirteenth that seems marginally better than the ones I had chosen the previous week. But the histories of two particular stocks have consistently ranked at or near the top of every list. I'm forced to put BerkshireHathaway "B" in the runners-up list, but it is one of my favorite DVolT trading and investing vehicles. (Symbol is commonly BRK/B, BRK-B or BRK.B). That really shouldn't be surprising. Over several decades good ol' Berky has been cobbled together by some of the sharpest minds in the investment world, the fabled tag team duo of Warren Buffet and Charlie Munger. They scout out easily understood companies with smart managers and great and reliably growing cash flows. BerkshireHathaway is more than just a stock. It is practically a legend. It is owned by thousands of investors who look upon Buffet and Munger with something like rock star awe. They understand what their managers do, have great confidence in their ability to perform and the shareholders are the type of people not apt to quickly sell in a downturn. (Unlike us!)

Stocks such as USSteel (X) General Electric (GE), though not on my list, are others everyone knows; old-school big caps with their DNA woven into the heart of America's industrial economy. Like BRK-B, they're not likely to pull a big earnings surprise and with so many institutional owners, violent stock movements tend to be unusual. You'll find some have moved with BRK-B in fairly close sympathy, though Berky has vastly out-performed many over the years.. Whenever you get a trade signal for one, you're fairly certain to get the same signal in the some other before long, which is a good thing. You'll find during much of your investing year you're either owning both of them or neither. Watch the list. Life gets simple, losses are minimized and gains get good.

I have never been able to find a pure-equity ETF of American stocks that is sufficiently low-volatility to trade with confidence. The best I have found are stock ETFs that are part bond, preferred or have some strategy applied to them. I have come up with FPE (preferreds), HNDL, TOTL and AOM. Even those are a bit more volatile than I like, so I put most in the B List for investors who feel they absolutely must have a widely diversified equity fund somewhere in their DVolT portfolio. In recent years AOM has quite closely tracked SPY, but with a less volatile chart. Compare them closely and I think you'll see fewer sudden plunges and leaps. I have never found any large cap tech stock that might behave with the DVolT calmness we seek, so for investors who want to be allocated in technology, I could not include FFTY, a tech-inclined fund of "disruptor" stocks highly rated by the respected Investors Business Daily. This ETF of exciting young companies has ironically lagged behind the broad market and AOM. It is marginal in terms of tradeable volatility.

-------------------.

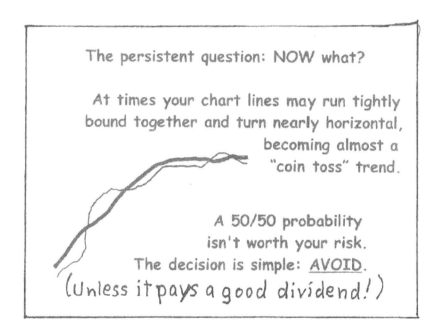

We have included PGP in our list, a most unusual bond-ish fund that gives its Pimco managers wide range to seek opportunities in markets of all kinds. They pack all manner of leverage and global debt instruments into this pony's saddle bags, and the best I can say is that Pimco managers have long-established reputations for knowing what they're doing, even if the fund has been a disappointment at times. It would be futile to even attempt explain how the managers deploy their assets as they are continuously seeking new inefficiencies and opportunities in all kinds of debt markets. That said, the PGP chart history has usually been as DVolT tradeable as we could ask for. Its chart type might change, but so far at the time of writing, it has a good chart personality for our purposes.

So there you have them: DVolT securities I currently use. I have no doubt the list will change over time. You will surely want to make your own list, but you now have a place to start. You now know what to trade and how to trade them, just as promised on the opening pages. But only you can test-trade the assets and test your own self-discipline to build success and confidence.

-------------------.

MEMO from ***The Stock Trader's Notebook:*** <u>**STOP!!**</u> ***This*** **is the moment to cease reading! Here's the point when you turn to your Yahoo! three-month chart, bleach out the price line and apply the 2- or 3-day moving average with a 15-day cross. Here's your first opportunity to go through the deep-volatility list one by one to decide for yourself if the charts are indeed eminently tradeable. Check out their histories. Does a new upward bend presage a profitable bull trend? (Or can you see how relatively little your loss would have been in the case of a head-fake?) Could you have gotten out in time when an upward-trending 2-day MA stalled and started to turn downward? Can you really understand the benefit of keeping abreast of your DVolT list to catch new bull or bear signals as they occur? Would you be more comfortable eliminating the P-SAR and just trade on your moving average crossovers? Do you agree that a two-line with bleach-out chart gives you better clarity? Can you visualize how much greater your gains are than losses if you trade your signals promptly?**

Like I wrote on the opening pages, don't just swallow my chatter – here's where you can damn well study your charts and

decide these questions for yourself. (And aren't you now glad your DVolT list is only about twenty five symbols?)

That's your homework assignment before you read another page. Do it.

---------------.

Let's think about this some more. If you're going to be a DVolT trader you're going to focus and gravitate toward a few funds and stocks for the same reason Willie Sutton heisted banks: because, as he said, "That's where the money is." You can search far and wide for new candidates if you like (and you probably should from time to time) but you must have a pretty compelling reason whenever you go wandering off the DVolT reservation. As you practice the protocol and get good at it, I predict you'll keep doing what works best. If you get into the habit of randomly searching for new DVolT trading candidates you should beware of adding any new fund just because it looks like it has a quiet history. You should also check it next to all the other stocks and funds already on your lists because there's little point in adding a fund if it closely tracks another fund you already have listed. When you find a close duplicate you might keep the new fund aside on a watch list if one of your main assets changes behavior and becomes untradeable. But adding fund after fund "just because" will actually hurt you eventually. To effectively practice your DVolT method, you'll be routinely combing through every security on your list to check its recent signals. The more funds you have on your list, the longer and more onerous your scanning chore will become, with the obvious risk that eventually you might not scan through your list quite so faithfully – and you will miss opportunities. Your asset list is short for a reason. Be sure of what you're doing when you add to it.

For investors lucky enough to be working with seven- or eight-figure portfolios, I can understand the hesitation they might feel in limiting their investment choices down to only twenty five possible candidates and five or six actual positions. They may have to force themselves to buy fewer positions in far larger quantities than feels comfortable. It might seem reckless to be so concentrated, even though it isn't. This is low volatility trading, I remind you. You'll be watching your positions like a hawk and will move whenever signals change. Your vigilance is your security. For these wealthy investors I suggest they start out applying DVolT to perhaps only 5 or 10% of their portfolio, and with the rest, just keep doing whatever they're used to. With time and careful attention, the wealthiest investors could do worse than to ease their way into the DVolT method and note how the system compares with the other investment "buckets" they are holding. You don't have to have a seven or eight-figure portfolio to slip your way cautiously into DVolT. Starting out taking baby steps may be just the ticket for large portfolios and small.

----------------------------.

MEMO from *My Stock Trading Notebook:* If you specialize in trading just a few DVolT assets, most days you will have no new signals and no trades to make at all..... and that's just what you should hope for. DVolT investors benefit most when their positions stretch out into long trends.

---------------------------.

Paper Trading and Kissing Your Sister Don't Count

Look, I get it. You want to paper trade DVolT to test it and see how it works for you. Great, you really must, but sooner or later you'll have to put your money on the table. I don't care if your first trades amount only to a couple of hundred-buck mini-purchases when you spot your first new buy signals. Real money, no matter how little, takes you to a whole 'nother level than paper trading with training wheels. And however your earliest forays turn out, you can't come to any conclusion from your first three or four investments. I know you'll be encouraged if all your first trades turn profitable, but the world isn't built that way. We deal in probabilities, not certainties. Character and determination really do count in this game and those you supply on your own. If you make the attempt to apply discipline and objectivity into your investing efforts I'm confident you will do very well indeed, but DVolT is a marathon, not a sprint.

---------------------.

MEMO from *The Stock Trader's Notebook:* After you have practiced the DVolT technique for a few months and gotten good at it, you might want to think about what you'll do with all your fat stacks and free time. After all, you could be one of those guys who can go up to his boss and say, "Yo, Mr. Finkel. Like to know what I really think of you ....?"

He'll probably call you a wise guy.

Dancing on the The Dark Side – and Loving It

The problem stumped me for ages when the solution was right in front of my nose. I wanted a deep-volatility bearish exchange traded fund (inverse ETF) to protect the dividend and income bucket in my portfolio when the market hit the skids, For months I kept coming back to look at the available bear ETFs, but they were impossibly volatile. Researching for this book, I knew we needed a big one to resort to when storm clouds rumbled. But as far as I can see there's nothing good enough out there. Of course to just buy and hold a big position in an inverse fund to hedge my losers in a bear market was just inviting trouble. The best I used to do was to dump big positions when "Sell!" signals were flashing and just go sit in cash for a while. Big cash couldn't lose money if the market went into a tailspin, but it certainly wouldn't make compensatory gains either. But cash was the cutest ugly gal in town.

And then it occurred to me --- if AOM behaves with relatively low volatility on the way up, might it also often show low volatility on the way down? If so, to hedge against the start of a bear market, I could sell short one of the calmest individual funds I know! – and that is what I started to do for portfolio protection when I needed it. I follow AOM all the time now, in bull and bear trends, using the same signals as before, letting short positions help buffer losses when my moving averages are slipping and I reverse back into bullish when trends begin to climb. It's like going from DRIVE to REVERSE and back. In the past the charts and moving averages when bearish, have been encouraging; still tending to move in the kind of slow-rolling waves I hope to see. AOM won't exactly trade perfectly inverse to SPY, but close enough and calm enough that I usually make gains and protect my principal when Mr. Market starts another s-storm. I feel sure one day I will get a nasty surprise from this pony. The market always surprises. But you might keep the short sides in mind. Logically a three-month chart turned upside down should work as well for AOM in bear markets as it does right-side-up when markets are bullish. Then again, life gets its buzz when logic and stock patterns break expectations.

So with the right tools finally at hand, we should try to anticipate the onset of any bear market as an opportunity rather than an inevitable calamity. When my signals sense the market heading south I generally will sell short small positions of AOM. I don't try to be aggressive and make money in a bear market; so far I just try to position myself to minimize overall net losses.

------------.

Stop-loss: – the trader's equivalent of a condom. It's something you know you should have used after it's too late.

--wallstreetjackass.typepad.com

------------.

How might you plan your Dark Side tactics? Here's a scenario that has worked for me. I am routinely tracking AOM on my usual 3 x 15 MA on a six-month Yahoo chart . One day I notice the SMI momentum is weakening and a couple of days later I get my "SELL" signal. Say I am holding 3000 shares of AOM. There is no time to think it out. I have already thought and planned. Now I act. I sell 2500 shares at once and then adjust my moving averages out to 5 x 25.

AOM keeps dropping. I am losing money on my remaining small hold, but my big initial sell prevents major losses. A week later the 5 x 25 flashes SELL also. I unload my remaining shares and then SELL SHORT another block of shares and re-set my moving averages to a sensitive 3 x 15 day moving average on a three-month chart

While this is going on over a period of weeks, I could be doing a similar continuous drill with BRK/B, for example. Working these two in harness smooths out contrary moments with the broader market and serves to stretch out the process into manageable steps, so long as I work with a purpose and do not delay. I feel going short BRK-B together with shorting AOM enjoys somewhat lower volatility and can be traded with less market-noise or "friction".

Please notice again, even with all my DVolT experience, my short positions are generally tiny next to my regular long allocations. I'm just not very aggressive when it comes to selling short in bear markets. When the bear growls, I don't seek big gains; I just want to protect my overall portfolio. That's the deal, O'Neal.

Here let's anticipate another objection; as AOM has a very low beta, some investors may object to using it, either long or short. If the market climbs 4% some week, you can expect AOM will generally rise only about 2% and similarly lag the S&P500 on the way down. Clearly you will more fully participate in market rallies if you hold SPY, FFTY or almost any other large and diversified all-stock fund. So why AOM? Simply because with it, you not only have an excellent chance to side-step any longer term bearish trends, but you can even profit from one by shorting AOM when signals indicate. *Suddenly participating in a Heads-I-Win/Tails-I-Win situation becomes a realistic possibility.* With AOM in your lineup you can look to gain in any market trend, so long as it isn't a head-fake, something next to impossible with a more volatile stock or ETF. Remember, AOM is your "ocean liner" ETF – easy for the alert D-VolT investor to enter when moving averages signal a new trend upward, and equally possible to exit and even to sell short when bear signals flash "sell". Such goals are next to impossible using SPY or almost any other all-equity fund.

Regardless of stock market directions, you can also simultaneously trade another win/win situation with the ying/yang TLT and TBF funds, which are moved by changes in long term interest rates and not by stock prices. The volatilities are manageable and I have had good success trading them back-and forth on slow-signal charts.

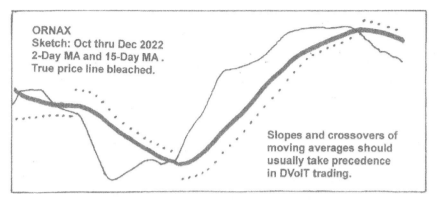

ORNAX
Sketch: Oct thru Dec 2022
2-Day MA and 15-Day MA .
True price line bleached.

Slopes and crossovers of
moving averages should
usually take precedence
in DVolT trading.

Another look how the PSAR can mislead, sending a false bullish
signal for days after a bull trend has already turned bearish.

---------------------.

**Warning! Selling short AOM or BRK/B probably isn't a good
idea for rookies. I'd feel better if you young'uns just go to cash
on any bear trend for your first six months or year of DVolT
trading. Get some real experience under your belt first.**

--------------------.

Desperately Seeking DVolT

Of course I'm never satisfied with my candidate list and you probably won't be either. I admit I spend too much time scanning charts like a pig for truffles, looking for other possible DVolT funds and usually conclude another fruitless search by deciding I have plenty enough assets to trade in the first place. I've tried to Google "low volatility stocks" and "low beta stocks" but the results are pretty useless. The first place you might think of are those ETFs like USMV, SPLV and FDLO. I've checked their charts many times and no dice; whatever these funds hold under the hood, the funds themselves are plenty too volatile for our purposes.

From time to time you may read claims that low volatility ETFs actually out-pace SPY on a longer term basis. I've looked into it and the notion doesn't seem to hold water. While it is true that such ETFs do pull ahead of SPY at times, their out-performance doesn't seem to last. On a buy-and-hold basis there are times when SPY will spurt ahead on longer term charts.

To seek new DVolT candidates with good technical charts and possible bullish prospects, I sometimes go to **stockcharts.com** and click on "MORE TOOLS" to find "PRE-DEFINED SCANS". Click on that and you can find "OVERSOLD WITH IMPROVING RSI". Click on THAT and you have your candidates to examine for low volatility. Other categories you can comb through on a quiet day are "NEW 52 WEEK HIGHS" "BULLISH MACDs" and even (you guessed it!) "PARABOLIC SAR BUY SIGNALS".

When searching for opportunities, I comb through those lists and "chart scan" every NYSE item on the list one by one. I might purchase a fund only if it appears DVolT <u>and</u> has recent upward MA lines, with the "fast" line above the "slow" line. (again, the 3 MA line is above the 15 MA line.). About 99% of the possibilities I scan never make the cut, which is OK. I have enough ponies in my stable. If not, something new usually comes trotting around the corner. And, as ever, for any asset I might buy, I will hold as long as moving average line continues upward or another indicator flips, and then sell at once when the first signal rings. No hand-wringing. No drama. Just sell.

Of course, in searching for new DVolT candidates you don't have to confine yourself to stocks you find on stockcharts.com. Nothing prevents you from taking a peek at any random security you happen to come across. Another step you can try is to google "Low Beta ETF List" (exactly those words in quotation marks) or you can google "Low Beta Stocks".

--------------------.

MEMO from The Stock Trader's Notebook: **Among its other features, TDAmeritrade's default 1-month and 3-month charts use a very good smoothing technology to reduce chart noise. Just add the P-SAR and/or 2 x 15 moving averages and you're well set to rock n' roll.**

-------------------------.

Did you know.....?

Traders of a deep volatility signal system would have avoided the Great Crash of 1929. I don't know if P-SAR had been figured out back then, but people surely understood moving averages and cross-overs – and they'd have been 100% in cash if disciplined. Since the market high of Sept 3, 1929, stocks had been stutter-stepping downward for well over a month. There can be no doubt anyone following technical signals would have been safely out of the market well before the carnage began. On October 24 Dick

Whitney made his famous walk across the stock exchange floor shouting out enormous buy orders to quell the rout. Many excited traders who saw him concluded the big banks were coming in to save the day, the crash would be over. Sadly, some bought eagerly into a brief but cruel dead-cat bounce that afternoon.

The following two days saw a nervous market, up a bit the 25th, down again the 26th. People had Sunday to mull it over, and many must have decided to hit the silk. Monday the 28th was genuine terror with the Dow tumbling 12%. The crash continued in earnest Oct 29th in free-fall right from the open. But disciplined technical traders who followed signals would not have been suckered in. They'd have been long gone to cash.

You may see a similarity with the Black Monday market crash of October 1987 which, on a one-day percentage drop was every bit as vicious as The Great Crash. The market reached its high early September 1987 then fell and mini-rallied the ensuing weeks. Prices stabilized at a relative high level the first couple of October trading days and then fell and fell for a good two weeks. Black Monday, October 19 saw the crash. The pre-market futures implied a somewhat weak opening, but as the first minutes after opening bell ticked by, the bearish momentum grew to a massive, unstoppable landslide. By one pm market maker specialists were refusing to answer their phones and were disappearing out to lunch. By two pm others were cowering under their desks, whimpering for mommy. Enormous computerized sell orders cascaded like colossal free-falling dominoes until there were no buyers left at all.

But anyone who carefully heeded charts, even on a hit or miss basis, escaped the worst. I know. I was there, a young married guy with a toddler to feed and hoping to buy a house. I wasn't at all systematic back then, but was already sniffing trend lines. I phoned my Dean Witter broker at 9:00 that morning and put in at-the-open, at-the-market sell orders on my biggest positions; the narrowest escape I ever had. But of course my big mutual fund couldn't be closed until the end of the day's trading. Sure, the fund eventually recovered, but I never forgot the body-blow I took that day. That was 35 years ago and I haven't owned a damned mutual fund since. It's one life lesson I never forgot – when I want to be out of a position, I want to be OUT.

My best friend from college had made a small fortune doing executive search around Silicon Valley. He retired in his 30s and went heavily into options. That morning he had been away from phones, out at a Florida drydock helping to refurbish a yacht he had just bought. By the time he learned what was happening it was too late. He couldn't meet his margin call that afternoon and was wiped out.

He kept the half-repaired yacht and wound up living on it; at night he had a great view of the Miami skyline. Financially, he never recovered.

The only time diligent DVolT traders would have been caught totally flat-footed was the 9/11 surprise attack tragedy of 2001. There was no warning whatever.

------------------.

MEMO from The Stock Trader's Notebook: A bull/bear tactical alternative: On broad market bullish trends, own VMFV. When reversing signals turn bearish, sell the VMFV and also sell short a smaller amount of AOM.

------------------.

Starting Your D-VolT Program – What You Can Realistically Expect

On your very first day, maybe even the entire first weeks of your D-Vol+T tryouts, you might do .... nothing. You will scan your D-Vol+T list over and again and you may see that half of your prospective assets are trending bearish, a couple are fluttering around on a flat, going-nowhere direction and any bullish funds might be marching upward on signals that are already two weeks old. You have to learn this important lesson, so you might as well learn it right at the start. *Chances are excellent on the first day – and on many days – you want to apply DVolT theory there will be nothing good to buy and nothing at all to do.* You may see every bullish stock or fund you are ready to trade has had no new buy signals for a month or more. Although you might scratch your rookie itch to take a small nibble on an old signal, you should never reach to buy a really big position on a stale indicator. Don't go chasin', Jason.

------------------.

This is the job. Don't wait for it to happen, don't even want it to happen. Just watch what does happen. --Jim Malone (played by Sean Connery) THE UNTOUCHABLES

------------------.

More possible start-up situations

Say you are starting with $15,000. Here is a possible scenario you might face and consider.

First, divide your $15,000 into three "buckets" of $5,000 each.

Eventually you will find two low volatility securities that show new or recent bullish signals. You buy them for $5000 each (call them A and B) and you leave $5,000 to remain in cash for a bit. If your buy signals are more than a week or two old, you buy only two very small positions, maybe just $2500 each instead of $5000.

A couple of days later you return to your portfolio and typically you might see one of your positions is up and one has slipped somewhat – however both are still overall trending upward with positive technical signals. What do you do? You do nothing. "Nothing" can be hard to do, but get used to it. Nothing is what winners do a lot.

A couple more days pass. Things are moving now. Your position A has gained more. Position B continues down a bit, but still maintains positive signals. Suppose then B drops more and now flashes a bearish P-SAR. You know what to do – but will you do it? You will be tempted to think, "Well, maybe it will bounce back" or "It's cheaper now. I should buy a bit more."

No. As soon as DVolT B throws off a new "sell" signal late in the day (probably a moving average cross) you must unload before the close of trading. The first time it happens to you – the first time you see an asset with a "buy" signal switching to a "sell" – is the moment for you to remember the first principles we discussed. We have already established that (like a large ocean ship) once it begins to change direction, probability favors it continuing in that new direction. Remember by the time you own an asset you're apt to form an opinion about it but you <u>must</u> disregard your feelings and heed your instruments. If you are using two signal systems, say the P-SAR and two moving average crossovers on the same chart, you might at the very least sell only half your position when you get the first signal, and sell out the rest if or when the second signal confirms.

Somewhere else a new "buy" signal will pop up in due time.

More To Expect on Your First Trades

When you make your first investments using D-VolT, remember another important fact. Simply because you identify a D-VolT pattern with promising potential does not mean you can anticipate a long, profitable bull trajectory every time. It merely means that the odds have probably turned somewhat in your favor. Maybe 35-40% of all bullish signals quickly revert back to bearish in a couple of days. That's a lot of little losers – but if so, it gives you 60-65% winners. But let's imagine worse. Suppose your winners run to only 50% of all your buys. In that case your discipline of "letting your winners run" should nevertheless make you more profitable than you have ever been before. You can anticipate brief but irritating little head fakes even during your longest and most profitable climbs. But small losses are all part of the game.

Though I've been disappointed by many, many bull signals that turned out to be headfakes, I have never had a serious loss from a disciplined DVolT trade.

It's never happened. Not once.

Frustrations: They're Baked Right In

When you have gained a little experience trading DVolT you will probably notice you are always buying your funds a little later than you could have and also you'll be selling a few days after you had your maximum gains. Along with any profitable sale will come the frustration of almost always "giving back" some of the gains you accumulated on its upward trend. For every hundred dollars you gain holding any one position, you can be assured you're probably going to "give back" ten or twenty or even sixty bucks when your signals flash SELL.

On the good days everything seems to click into place. Your positions move as you intended, almost pre-planned and tightly synchronized. But serendipity cannot last. One of your charts seems to stall or shows signs of topping out. Maybe the market opens with a surprise and you have five upward-trending positions that have all slipped downward in the first half hour of market trading, though no signals have changed. You feel the urge to do something. You yearn to ACT. You want to fix your uncertainty and sell something. You'd go back to yesterday if you could. But there is only one thing to be done. You may face anxious hours when your trajectories appear to be sputtering, but you haven't seen a SELL signal yet. So grit your teeth, clench your fists, or anything else you have to do, but **do nothing** unless a late hours sell signal appears.

DVolT trading is a discipline to use probabilities in your favor, to own winning positions and to trade so winners outnumber losers, and that your poor choices lose less than your winners gain. You're not swinging for the fences here, but you are getting on base – a lot. Frustration is a worthless emotion. DVolT has no room for "shoulda, woulda". Pocket your gains and get over it.

Think About Managing Money

We have already established what the competent DVolT investor does when a position he or she holds flashes a "sell" signal. But what will you do if your stock goes up from your initial buy price, and continues going up? There has been a lot of hand-wringing chatter about this issue. One prominent and successful investor I know has encouraged continual aggressive buying as a stock climbs, calling his theory "pyramid up".

While we believe a buyer enjoys favorable odds when a low-volatility asset triggers a buy signal for the first time, we're unable to quantify that advantage. If FTF has been falling for several weeks, finds support at around 12 and begins to turn upward, triggering a P-SAR buy signal at 13.00, are your odds of reaching 15 a 7-10 probability? 8-10? 52-100? We don't know and it may be impossible to determine in any particular case. But what seems likely for the repeat-buying investor is that his final incremental buy or two will be losers. Nothing goes up forever.

I'm not going to object if you make repeated purchases while on the way up, but experience seems to indicate that your first buy or your confirming bull signal buy should be your largest. When I make additional buys on a bull trend those subsequent trades are rarely larger than 5% or 10% of my confirming buy. I don't have an argument for any particular size of subsequent buys. My 10% limit is just something I do that seems to work. Plan your trades and trade your plan – and before you make any investment, know how why you're going to get in and how you'll get out.

Security Analysis For Beginners
or
DIY Dentistry You Can Do At Home With A Power Drill and Pliers

Library shelves groan with tomes authored by investment experts insisting that you must learn to do your own deep research into equities you buy. But why would you try if you're probably never going to be much good at it? Benjamin Graham's classic SECURITY ANALYSIS (currently in its sixth edition) runs some 700 pages. You could try to study it, or you might get an MBA to qualify you to really dig into the high weeds of a big company's annual report and likely wind up agreeing with a hundred analysts and disagreeing with a hundred others.

As we discussed in the opening pages, many small investors rely on recommendations put out by the analysts working for various news programs or investment firms. Analyst ratings shoveled out free to the public are often just pablum to encourage us to trade, so tread suspiciously here. You probably wouldn't buy a stock if a Merrill Lynch or Goldman Sachs analyst rates it underperform. But you must allow that A) expert analysts often disagree among themselves and (B) when analysts do agree, it's often too late for you to take advantage of their information and (C) sometimes these enormously smart and qualified people end up just wrong. And if they can't get it reliably right, what realistic chance have we? Case in point: In February 2022 the widely monitored and constantly analyzed Facebook stock suffered a deep, sudden collapse. Hardly a single analyst had warned the public about upcoming risk in that high-flyin' FB. But – oh boy – did they ever crowd in with their "sell" recommendations the day <u>after</u> FB plunged! I mean, c'mon. It's embarrassing to have your "buy" recommendation hanging out there on the 'net for a stock that has just cratered. (The expression "CYA" comes to mind.) A couple of months later, on April 18 2022 Netflix reported it was losing subscribers. Shareholders woke up to disaster the next morning, finding their position had evaporated some 35% overnight with hardly any warning from the analysts.

Don't despair. If you can't become a top-notch stock analyst and if many recommendations are out of date, there are still some simple street-smart tactics any wise guy can use. Years ago when I was new to investing I read somewhere to disregard any stock analysis opinion more than a month old and that newly published analyst opinions were hardly much better. The trick, I remember reading, was to look for <u>brand new upgrades or downgrades of previously published opinions.</u> You might also look for consensus. A sole analyst's opinion feels more reliable if ten other analysts agree with him. Or it may again just be a case of everyone following the CYA herd.

Let's go back to you in the balloon watching the ship. After spotting the ocean liner change course did you do a stock analysis of that particular ship? Of course not. When the ocean liner starts to alter its course, you know practically nothing about it. If you knew it was carrying wheat or coffins or artillery shells or cut roses or computer parts, you might be able to get a better fix on what port it was heading for. But you're in a balloon, not in an ideal scenario. You don't have the manifest. That information is tricky to get if you're soaring free 2000 feet over an ocean. But right there, at that moment you do have your eyes fixed on the start of its course change. If you had the up-to-date security analysis or insider information, you might make a more precise prediction. But we can learn to work effectively with just the limited real-world knowledge at hand. All you have at that moment is a probability. And in quantity, probabilities are enough.

MEMO from *The Stock Trader's Notebook:*

You don't need to prognosticate where a stock or the entire market will be next month or next year. With DVolT discipline you only need to have a clear fix on how your asset is trending right now. Suddenly life becomes much simpler and investing more profitable.

Still, if you're never going to be a professional level securities analyst, it's certainly worth your while to learn to use a few basic analytic tools you have at hand and have a website or two that will give you a respectable information panel for a stock you're curious about. Fidelity, Schwab, TDAmeritrade do a good job in this regard. Merrill Lynch features an extremely useful and user-friendly research device. Call up any well known stock symbol and click on their "STOCK STORY" button. Up pops a very clearly designed series of critical fact boxes about that company – one after another.

I also really like **finviz.com**. Go to their home page and plug in almost any well known stock symbol and you will get a detailed data panel – all on one page – giving you the performance data you're most likely to want. Couldn't be simpler. I especially like to compare their present earnings per share (EPS) with their estimated EPS for the upcoming year. Obviously this gives you a decent indication if the company is likely to grow earnings. Then I compare the EPS with the dividends the company is paying to indicate if the firm is earning enough to actually afford its distributions.

Beginning investors still learning to evaluate companies will find almost all the performance numbers they're likely to want, like ROE (Return on Equity) Operating Margin, Inside Ownership, Analyst Consensus and more, all neatly laid out on one screen. DVolT investors will find another handy bit of data if they search the far lower right of the data panel and note finviz even rates the volatility amount for every stock. As far as I know, finviz is unique in giving you a complete list of recent inside buyers, then they go a step further by highlighting the important large inside buys in a bold green background and the less important small buys in a pale green background.

Yes, this is certainly simplistic. A panel of finviz numbers are nothing like an in-depth, competent analysis, but it does give you a place to start, and if you uncover some mystifying contradictions, you may just 1 look elsewhere.... or you might keep digging and keep learning.

Case in point: I always admired Carl Icahn and a while back I was thinking about buying Icahn Enterprises stock (symbol: IEP). Icahn has gained fame and fortune over the years for accumulating opportunistic positions in businesses and then encouraging changes (twisting arms, perhaps?) to increase shareholder value. Well, first off I saw finviz gave IEP a top-notch analyst consensus of 1. OK. So far so good. But then I see the performance numbers for IEP look like a big, steaming bowl of weird. Finviz reports IEP lost 1.63 per share this year and only projects making .87 next year. So how, one wonders, do they expect to continue paying their $2.00 annual dividend except out of their enormous cash hoard of $20/share? A possible contradiction? Then I see Icahn Associates owns 89% of the company valued at $14 billion. Clearly here's a man who eats his own cooking.

For another analysis I go to TDAmeritrade's TipRanks/SmartScore that ranks many stocks on a sliding scale of 1 to 10. What I appreciate here is that the scores are updated daily. Whatever limitations lurk in TipRanks scoring software, the information isn't stale. (In TipRanks' case 1 is the worst, whereas 1 is the best with finviz.) TipRanks gives IEP their top drawer 10. Don't forget Zacks, which does a relatively competent job of up-to-date analysis too. It's fairly basic, hardly sophisticated, but still good to have at hand. Lastly I go to seekingalpha.com to check to see if they have published any recent articles on IEP. After every article, there's an open forum of comments and criticism about the article you've just read – and often the sharp criticisms are well worth the read. My last step; check the charts and the signals. IEP isn't exactly deep volatility, but the chart looks good and signals bullish. Clearly there's more to this company than the average small investor will readily comprehend, but with enough resources at hand, I can see and understand enough to make a small, considered purchase.

Let the MBAs tsk-tsk and the analysts chuckle. With your DVolT discipline and readily available resources, you can out-perform the **whole dern bunch. No one sneers at you in the Benz dealership.**

------------------.

THE TWO RULES OF MARKET FORECASTING

-Rule 1: For each forecast, there is an equal and opposite forecast.

-Rule 2: Both of them are wrong.

--Bill Berger

Why we repeat investing mistakes: The Ebbinghaus Forgetting Curve postulates that in 48 hours you have forgotten up to 70% of your experiences.

------------------.

A Few Basics About Closed End Funds (and the clever pros who manage them)

Whole books are written about closed end funds. Online discussion groups go red with blood spilled feuding over them. While closed end funds are not central to our trading method, there are a few basics every small investor should know.

Many inexperienced people, especially retirees, seek reliable income from their investments and when some of them discover closed end funds (CEFs) it's like a "Ka-Ching!" bell goes off in their heads. *"Just look at those big beautiful yields! So much better than mutual funds and most ETFs. This is what I've always searched for."*

Well, that's the moment to think "uh oh". Because while they appear simple and straight-forward, closed end funds can be complicated little critters. Some people call a CEF "a wrapper of assets" to remind us that its price doesn't depend only on the value of its underlying parts but to some extent on the fickleness of small investors. Just knowing they are favored by retail investors more than by large institutions gives you reason enough to tread carefully here. Many closed end funds are moderately leveraged (OK, so what?) but you should also know many closed end funds are not actually earning those big, luscious distributions they're shelling out.

How's that again? I said: a lot of them <u>pay out more than they're actually earning</u>.

That's a situation you should understand. In many cases it's hard to find a clear answer to a CEF's real earnings/payout ratio, which often lies buried in arcane reporting documents well beyond the pay grade of your average small investors.

If I am considering purchase of a CEF, the first thing I want to know, on a dollar-in/dollar-out basis is: are the distributions sustainable? (IOW, is it really earning enough to keep paying the investors?) One sponsor that regularly and clearly publishes numbers on how well their incomes cover their distributions is PIMCO. To find out the latest "coverage ratios" on their different CEFs you need to go to Google and search "Pimco UNII". (UNII stands for Undistributed Investment Income). Their reports that come out around the middle of every month are clear and timely. It is especially interesting to compare each monthly report to the previous to see which Pimco CEFs are gaining UNII month over month. (Howzat?) If my CEF distributes 12 cents monthly and it had a UNII of .23 on its books last month and a new UNII of .34 this month, the fund is clearly earning more than it is paying out. If the good news continues, it is a candidate for an increase in monthly distributions or a happy surprise end-of-year special dividend.) Closed end funds are obligated to pay out most of their earnings every year, unlike corporations which may hoard cash if management wishes. It would be nice if all CEF earnings reports were as transparent as Pimco's. But they're not.

To complicate CEF matters further, closed end funds operate on two separate prices. There's the underlying value of the fund (called "Net Asset Value" or NAV) and the actual trading prices you're quoted on the internet – and the two prices are often very different! Popular CEFs often sell at a "premium" meaning you have to pay more than the fund's assets are actually worth – or the fund might be trading at a discount (the fund's underlying assets are worth more than you are actually paying).

You can easily see whether a CEF is trading premium or discount by looking it up on **cefconnect.com**. Cefconnect also puts out a chart telling where the fund's distributions are coming from. I have to say a lot of investors doubt those published numbers. I don't have an opinion, but you can at least go to their "Regular Distribution Type" line. If it says "Managed Distributions" the CEF is admitting it's paying out whatever the managers want to. But if it says "Income Only" you can probably guess managers are at least trying to match payouts with income. But no promises from me.

Now you might think it's a big no-no to pay a premium for any CEF, but sometimes the fund is premium-priced because investors have great confidence in it. Small discounts or premiums (actually the correct plural is "premia") don't generally mean very much. But if a CEF is sporting a big premium, say over 10% or so, you might think to look elsewhere until the premium shrinks a bit.

Let's look a little deeper. Let's say you own a CEF that is not fully earning its distributions, but the investment managers are clever and the NAV is steadily rising. Well that's a good thing. The managers can make up the shortfall in their earnings by steadily peeling off tiny little bits of the gains they're accumulating and pay some of those gains out as part of their regular distributions. We call this "Return of Capital" or ROC.

But this works well only so long as the NAV is climbing. If NAV stalls or, worse yet, starts to slide, there are no new gains to sell off and management eventually has to either (A) cut the distributions or (B) sell off the underlying assets bit by bit to maintain the illusion they're still earning the full dividend. CEF managers don't ring a little bell when they're forced to switch from paying off bits of gains to feeding you their seed corn.

Let's have a simple illustration. Imagine there's a CEF (symbol: DUMB) with just one underlying holding, the cigarette company MO. (Spare me your howls. We're talking theory here. Pay attention, Gretchen.) Now to boost its distribution (to make it popular for small investors) the CEF employs 20% leverage.

Huh? The CEF raises $10 million and borrows $2 million and buys $12 million worth of MO. (OK, so it's a really small CEF,) We know that MO stock pays a big yield, say about 8%, but since it is leveraged an extra 20%, the CEF managers can pay out 120% of 8%, or about 9.6% before interest and management expenses. Not bad, we think.

But this is CEF-land and management is aggressive. They REALLY want you to buy and drive up the price of their fund. They believe MO is going to be climbing in price and they bet they can use the increasing NAV to pay out …. 12% !

And that's the first thing you see combing through lists of closed end funds:

Symbol:DUMB
Type:Equity
Price10.50
NAV10.80
Yield:12%
Regular Distribution TypeManaged Distributions

"Holy Moses!" you think. "I gotta buy some!" Now under this scenario you're probably going to be happy as long as MO (the underlying NAV) keeps rising. Management can keep peeling off small amounts of shares as the stock climbs and the NAV stays solid, or even rises while you feel brilliant, getting your 12%.

But MO doesn't have to fall for the DUMB fund to start deteriorating. It just has to find a steady plateau and your investment will start leaking (the fund is constantly paying you more than MO dividend is paying them, remember?) If they keep paying while MO has stopped rising, you get into a situation known as "Destructive ROC" – and those 12% distributions are a mirage which will eventually come back to bite you. Better be sellin', Ellen.

One additional wrinkle: some CEFs will invest in dividend-paying assets and attempt to boost that income by selling options on its underlying positions. I have always felt that the money derived from selling options is part of the fund's income from operations, but in their reports such distributions are generally accounted as ROC. I can't explain it, but there it is.

In simplest terms, how can you tell if a closed end fund is earning its distributions? A generally reliable way is to go to cefconnect.com and look at the fund's NAV chart. If the NAV is generally rising, that's a pretty fair indication that the distributions are being supported either by earnings or gains. If NAV is trending bearish, well ….. you get the drift. But it's not always that straightforward. For the first six months of 2022 the closed end fund PDI was steadily losing NAV, not to mention it was also going lower and lower in trading price. Nevertheless Pimco's monthly reports showed PDI was greatly out-earning its monthly payouts and UNII kept climbing. How were the Pimco elves able to out-earn their generous distributions on a mortgage and debt CEF while at the same time lose NAV? And if earnings were so excellent, why were investors continually selling and selling?

As we've seen, (1) CEFs can be complicated, (2) some managers are more adroit than others and (3) investors are frequently irrational. There you have it.

-----------------.

ASIDE: If you are going to invest regularly in closed end funds for their big distributions, you might consider using schwab.com as a brokerage. They have developed a handy little display for a great many CEFs that breaks down the sources of payouts by percentages: income, long term capital gains, short term capital gains and return of capital. With so many CEFs comprised of a myriad of moving investment parts, leveraging and hedging, you might not take the schwab.com reported numbers as absolute gospel. Their little CEF data panel is certainly simplistic, but you might find it pretty handy.

For your pay grade, the takeaway is that CEFs are little understood by the mostly small investors who trade in them. An eroding NAV is never good news, but you're probably not going to be wounded too badly if management can consistently out-earn their payouts. So we return to first principles. You are probably never going to understand all the risks and machinations your CEF managers go through to pay those big yields, real or imagined. With many Pimco funds, for example, we're talking exotic trading flora like leverage ratios, sophisticated options spreads and collateralized loan obligations ... not to mention reverse repurchase agreements and credit default swaps. So if the typical retail investor is going to own a CEF, s/he absolutely must heed its longer term chart! Whether you understand it or not, there might be a good reason why that lush 12% yielding CEF is steadily falling in price, and when that happens, you need to be .... gone. Whether from the fearful fickleness of mass crowd psychology or a flaw in management's investment operations, you never want to be on the wrong side of a declining price chart, regardless of the distributions.

----------------------.

"Planning is important, but the most important part of every plan is to plan on the plan not going according to plan." The Psychology of Money --Morgan Housel

---------------------.

A Closed-End Love Tragedy

Poets sing of springtime and romance. And so it was for me. The cold winds of late March 2022 softened into the first gentle breezes of early April, and I was head-over-heels in love with PDI and PDO, two famous closed end funds in the Pimco family. Fool that I was, I couldn't help my infatuation. Each had its own inspiring story. PDI had just renewed itself by folding two other famous funds, the former PKO and PCI, within it, making PDI a giant powerhouse among CEFs, able to deploy new economies of scale. And bright, perky PDO was a brand new fund, an eager filly just bursting to run rings around her bigger, muscular cousin. Both funds were paying big monthly distributions and both were actually earning far more than they were paying out.

Best yet, both of these funds had fallen from their highs. An early April buy of little PDO would garner me a steady income stream of 9.5% and big, bad PDI was tossing off over 10%, and both were earning so strongly, there was already a good chance of special end-of-year extra dividends. What was there not to love?

Except – all my indicators kept flashing a steady "avoid". Week after week, despite all logic and data, PDI and PDO followed the general market down and down. After several generally quiet decades, inflation was rearing its ugly head like it had in the 1970s and 80s. Well, what of it? I felt sure Pimco investment managers were some of the best in the world. Surely they forgot more about inflation than I'll ever know. They MUST have adjusted for it and were profiting from it with their complicated swaps and hedges (stuff I barely understood in their reports) as their stellar earnings numbers showed. But the market didn't care.

Everything I knew and felt about investing told me to buy these puppies, but my signals persisted in flashing "avoid". So I avoided. Of the two funds, PDO appeared to have lower volatility, so that's where I concentrated my attention and watched as it stutter-stepped its way down from about 20 in January 2022 to around 15 the third week in May, when I finally got my "Buy!" signals. And by mid-June I was buying big heaping fistfuls around 14 and wrote about it in a couple of my discussion groups.

This again is how technical indicators can rescue you from your errors. Moving average cross-overs can even save you when your thinking is correct but the market is irrational and your timing is off! And the market, as old timers say, can stay crazy longer than you can remain solvent.

EPILOGUE. Though it seemed that love had triumphed in the end, it was not to be. Hardly a week passed before my PDI and PDO continued ....dropping! Down again, down again. Jiggity-jig. Against all logic, earnings and facts, their little bull rally had turned into a head-fake and we were compelled to tearfully part again when they continued to steadily drop with the rest of the market. As I write this, PDI has now fallen from a high of around 26 to under 19.00 while PDO continues bumping downward from a New Years high around 20 to 13.60 nine months later – and they're still searching for a bottom.

Moral #1: Love your mother, love your puppy, love your kids – but never love a stock.

Moral #2: Dividends be damned. Never own on the way down.

--------------------.

MEMO from *The Stock Trader's Notebook:* **On the seekingalpha.com website there's a regular and highly respected contributor who writes under the title "Stanford Chemist". He puts out a monthly essay entitled The Quality Closed-End Fund Report with an analysis of various CEFs which are all over-earning their distributions. Worth the read.**

--------------------.

Some other authors I follow on SeekingAlpha.com are

Peter F. Wray

Colorado Wealth Management

HFIR

Nick Akerman

Douglas Albo

Guido Persichino

Alpha General Capital

Arbitrage Trader

Scott Kennedy

Lyn Alden Schwartzer

Juan de la Hoz

Tip: I find it's a red flag when an author comes out with too many analyst articles. Wise guys suspect no one can possibly discover great & legitimate new investment ideas three times a week.

----------------.

Divvies and Distribs – a Few Words

Don't talk to me about your dividend investing, chump. I was a yield junkie when Moses was in short pants. I had a PIMCO tat on my left cheek. I used to send valentines to Bill Gross. So if you think dividends and interest make important streams of income into your portfolio, you'll get no back-sass from me. But there is such a thing as chasing unrealistic yields and over-doing it. I've seen and joined battles royale over the proper role of distributions in a portfolio and I return to PDO history as my case study.

Again, in late 2021 PDO was the hot new fund in the news. It had been throwing off about 9% in monthly distributions (almost twelve cents a share) and had also paid a nifty special dividend around Christmas that year. The only fly in the ointment was that its trading price, as we've seen, had been a little weak, slipping from about 20.50 in October to about 19.50 around New Years.

Now with closed end funds, there's such a thing as the "January effect" which all the old-timers know about and many use. The theory works like this: say you're watching a good CEF that has dropped somewhat in a slipping market. A lot of small investors are apt to sell that fund late in the year to reap some losses for their tax returns, so it's very likely to drop more in early December, even though it's a good fund. The tax-loss selling typically heats up around Thanksgiving and ends around Christmas time, as opportunistic buyers will often start to rush in when the CEF appears near its lowest. January is typically an excellent month for such CEFs. Well, that's what usually happens.

Anyway, this gambit had worked for me before so I went to the well one more time and started buying PDO early December, but a funny thing happened: PDO kept dropping all the way through New Years and inexplicably into January. I quickly sold it, bewildered and with a small loss. Dumb fund. Too young and stupid to know it was supposed to climb. Well, several discussions popped up on the internet about it. I was criticized for not understanding investing long term for income. A few months later their heated argument boiled down to, "Hey, if you have a good fund that's earning a generous yield, you should be indifferent to price fluctuations. The only thing that really matters is maintaining your excellent long-term dividend stream."

To me this made no sense. "Look," I answered, "you own PDO which you bought for about 20.00 last October. I bought in December, saw my error, and sold it in January because it was falling. I can re-purchase it any time. Six months later, in late June, it's down below 15.00. In that time it's paid about 12 cents per month in distributions. You've collected eight distributions for roughly 96 cents plus 37 cents in a special December dividend but you've <u>lost</u> five bucks in principal. I collected one distribution and one special dividend and lost about 40 cents in principal. And you think you're *ahead?*" (We'll draw the veil of decorum over the convo that followed.)

Avoiding large losses is key. <u>In the end, the only things that really matter are your total returns (dividends PLUS gains or losses) and the risks you take to get them.</u> Even among educated and intelligent investors, there's often some kind of goofy arithmetic illiteracy afoot which would be rather amusing if it didn't cost money. Holding a steadily swooning stock for its dividends is a sucker's bet. You never know how low a falling stock will drop. Some people do seem to go blind when they defend their dividends and opinions.

Mind your chart, Bart.

`Here's an actual message publicly sent to me by a well-known writer on seekingalpha.com after I argued not to buy a certain bearish-trending company for its dividend. Wait and buy the stock, I said, when its falling price finds support. The author replied:

"You know nothing about income investing. You watch your little talking heads on CNBC who follow stock markets the way ESPN does sports, getting millions of people addicted to the hourly, daily, weekly, etc. movements of stock prices like its some sort of soccer match or football game. That's how the media makes its money. Price is everything; "total return" - which is what really matters - well, to them, that's not so important. Why? Because they can't track it minute to minute, like prices.

Whereas real economists and investors have known for generations that over the long term what gives stocks, bonds, buildings and other assets their ultimate value is the cash income they produce over their lifetimes.

But don't let facts or history deter you. Go ahead and play with your little charts and have a good time."

This is a typical retort when I suggest applying objective DVolT tactics to a falling stock. Note the hostility in his reply, a common attitude when a person's opinions are challenged with technical facts. The nay-sayer almost never debates what I've just suggested. He invariably invents something I DIDN'T say and argues against that. I'll state that "total return" should be the goal and he'll reply, "NO! Total <u>return</u> is the most important!" I will argue that dividend stream in a collapsing stock is a net loss and he will ignore the "collapsing stock" part as if it didn't exist and often drags out the old canard *"It's not really a loss until you sell it."* I'll even agree his readers might buy the damn stock if it makes them happy, but only when it stops dropping. He ignores that too.

In other places I have been advised not to publish my DVolT

theory, claiming a book discussing my ideas would be "unethical"! (Yes, that's the word they used.) Elsewhere I have been threatened with a liability lawsuit.

Yes, some people get REALLY bothered when a new theory challenges their long-held notions.

-------------------------.

Commodities Without Tears

By the way, from time to time you might want to check commodity funds. They often move contrary to the market, so they're a good potential diversifier. (Note: "POTENTIAL"). Just know that many of these funds issue a K-1 which can complicate your tax reporting. If you're skilled at doing your own tax returns, it's no biggie, but a minor level headache for the rest of us knuckleheads.

For commodity exposure without the K-1 baggage, look to SDCI, COMB, PDBC or BCI. In August 2022 a new no-K1 agricultural commodity fund emerged, PDBA. In our time of rapidly rising food prices, these funds may be worth keeping in mind.

I also like DBMF, a multi-asset ETF with a managed futures strategy; particularly good for its low correlation with bond or equity markets. Where ever other markets go, DBMF tends to march to its own drummer. Its website says it "seeks to replicate the pre-fee performance of leading managed futures hedge funds and outperform through fee/expense disintermediation ...... The fund seeks long-term capital appreciation. The fund will employ long and short positions in derivatives, primarily futures contracts and forward contracts, across the broad asset classes of equities, fixed income, currencies and commodities." (Whew.)

Do I recommend you go out and buy DBMF? I certainly do not. But if you still have an eye for diversification, or an ETF that might veer left when the market jukes right, here's a fund to keep in mind.

"DVolT means never having to say you're sorry, PREPPIE."

Doin' The DCA Twist

Dollar Cost Averaging is often a mental refuge for those masochists who refuse to stop buying on the way down, and we must admit there's a kind of twisted logic to it. If XXX looks interesting at 20 I should really like it at 19 which makes it a great buy at 18 and a terrific bargain at 17 – and so on. The unspoken assumption in this train of thought as you continue accumulating shrinking shares is that the bottom MUST be close at hand, utterly ignoring the what-if-I'm-wrong principle. Stocks can and do swoon down to pennies and are kicked off their exchange to languish forever on the pink sheets. The unmistakably ugly part of DCA is you have a plan for getting into a falling stock, but none for getting out. DCA doesn't ask if earnings are cratering or executives are resigning like rats from a sinking barge. It just looks at price. If you mis-judge the bottom, you have no stop-loss unless or until you capitulate and swallow big losses indeed.... something that should never happen with DVolT!

-------.

Think your stock can't fall any lower? (This just in: Hell has a basement.)

-------.

But let's keep an open mind. Maybe there's a way to make DCA work after all. Let's set DVolT aside for a sec and consider something else. First of all, suppose we restrict ourselves to only ETFs and CEFs that are fully earning their payouts. Add to that only the best quality dividend-paying, profitable stocks we can find.

If you're determined to DCA your way into something (and I don't suggest you do!) you absolutely cannot be cavalier with your choices.

OK, you find a profitable stock paying a nice 7% dividend. TipRanks likes it. Finviz and Zacks like it. All the analysts rate it "Buy". You buy at 30. But it falls in a bear market and you buy more at 28 and again at 26. Say it finds support at around 24. You make your (hopefully final!) buy at 24.

My opinion: four DCA buys on the way down is your absolute limit. If you are wrong about this stock, you must have at least some self discipline to protect yourself from a knock-out punch.

Then say your stock rallies, at last, to 26. At this point you might assume a last-in-first-out attitude and you SELL the final tranche you bought at 24 for a nice little two-buck gain. After that your stock bounces around 26, going essentially nowhere for a while and you just hold for the dividend. If it eventually climbs to 28, you sell another tranche for a second $2 gain, but if it falls back down to 24, you can re-buy the last tranche you sold at 26. We're assuming that if you once loved your top-quality stock at 24, you should still love it the second time it drops that low. And so you continue, taking bite-sized gains when your stock rallies and re-buying added trenches on dips .... but never more than four buys and NOTHING below 24. Ever.

Of course if none of the above happened, if your $30 buy soars to $120, you might do a few little buys on the way up, but the problem has solved itself.

Am I recommending this dollar cost averaging procedure? Hell, no. I remain implacably against any buys on the way down, but if you must have that loser-stock or fund via DCA, you will now at least have a plug-ugly working plan for limiting your losses. If your stock continues dropping from your final-buy price of 24, you simply must reverse course, bite the bullet, and sell a bucket of it in steps on each lower dollar drop. By this time you're flailing around, reduced to "hope" mode. "Hope" is no investment plan, bubba. Eat your losses and look elsewhere, the next time with more discipline and fewer emotions. If you make a bone-head blunder you must at least avoid catastrophe to survive and profit another day.

After all that, there yet remains a strong case when dollar cost averaging is entirely appropriate. We're talking about young people starting out in their careers with nothing in the bank, those with new families who have little interest in the stock market. In such cases, and there are many, an automatic monthly deduction into a dividend- paying equity fund makes good sense. To begin such a program at age 23 and continuing until early retirement at 53 gives you 360 investment deposits you might make with nary a thought to the ups and downs of stock markets. Such habits of thrift have long been a royal road to comfort and security later in life. Historically, consistent DCA over decades of time has been an unbeatable plan for people with interests elsewhere. You have no promises for the future, but for millions, the plan has worked well in the past.

-------------------------.

MEMO from *The Stock Trader's Notebook:*"If you remember nothing else, remember this. Stock or mutual fund selection is not nearly as important to your success in the stock market as is the direction of the overall market. Statistics show that when the market moves strongly in either direction, it carries roughly 75 percent of stocks with it."

----Sy Harding in "Riding The Bear"

-------------------.

A finger in the wind: sensing The Big Picture

Is the "wind at your back" with a favorable environment for being fully invested? Or is the tide flowing against you and should you go at least partly into cash?

You can read a dozen conflicting commentators about where the market will be, chattering away online every market day. But in the end, nobody knows jack. In truth, we no longer need to listen to opinions, ours or anyone else's. We can remain disciplined and heed our charts for a crystal clear overall view of present market trends. Here's how:

Back to Yahoo charts, guys. Just for grins, step outside your comfort box again and try me here. (It should be easy by now.)

1. Go to yahoo.com and click on FINANCE

2. Enter AOM and click on CHARTS

3. Where you see DATE RANGE, click on 1Y for ONE YEAR and where you see 1D Interval change it to 1 WEEK

4. In the upper left of the chart click on the little box that says AOM

5. An inset box pops up. Click on the color sample and select a VERY FAINT light gray. (Bleach it out. You know the drill, Bill.) Return to the chart.

6. Click on INDICATORS and scroll down to MOVING AVERAGES. Click on it. Where it says 50, change it to 3 and return to the chart. Click on INDICATORS a second time, scroll again to MOVING AVERAGES. Where it says 50 change it to 20 this time.

Here's a chart to give you clues for market climate:

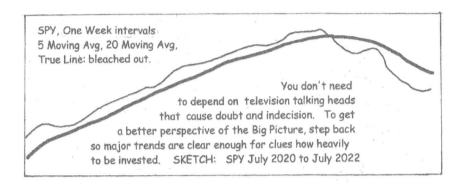

SPY, One Week intervals
5 Moving Avg, 20 Moving Avg,
True Line: bleached out.

You don't need
to depend on television talking heads
that cause doubt and indecision. To get
a better perspective of the Big Picture, step back
so major trends are clear enough for clues how heavily
to be invested. SKETCH: SPY July 2020 to July 2022

What you see -- again -- the true chart line has all but disappeared. Now it's replaced by the much smoother 3 Week Moving Average that loosely tracks it.

The **slope** of your slow 20-Week Moving Average will give you an overall picture of a bullish or bearish environment,. If the lines are trending up, you probably should be heavily invested, especially when the fast 3-Week line is trending above the slow 20-Week. Regard the slopes as your reference to cut through all the talking heads of the television and internet experts. Specific funds or stocks aside, this long-view chart helps decide if you really want to be invested heavily.

Any time you see your 3-Week MA slip under the 20-Week MA is your general warning to take some chips off the table, and keep them off. With this longer term chart in your tool bag, the continuous cacophony of pundits barking their conflicting market predictions should never again distract you.

Using the DVolT advantage you can be an active trader or you can be a longer term investor. But I won't let you be a loser.

-------------------.

"Our job is to find a few intelligent things to do, not to keep up with every damn thing in the world." --Charlie Munger

-------------------.

We Don't Have Opinions. We Have Observations.

Market direction is a never-ending topic in the media and on the better online investing forums like Mutual Fund Observer, Big Bang Investors, Fidelity Investor Community, Morningstar Discussion Group, Armchair Investors and seekingalpha.com. No one on these forums is going to argue against the certainty that some investors have better financial education and expertise than others. In the better forums, when the "smart money" guys and gals wander into the deep waters of some esoteric debate, other posters generally step aside and keep mum. If conversations devolve to the fine print of "Is short term bond fund xyzx superior to short term bond fund xyax?" many feel they have nothing to add, particularly when the investment pros appear to be debating solely for the sheer love of exercising their abilities. It is human nature to enjoy participating in our best skills, be they tennis, alpine skiing or security analysis. Nevertheless, at times I suspect some of the best educated experts can't see the forest for the enormous oak or maple in front of their nose.... as they argue whether it is best to walk around a tree on the left side or the right. Most professional investors develop mighty opinions on the smallest of issues and defend them no matter how irrelevant to real life they may be. It's not a criticism -- debating theory in areas of expertise is an important exercise for those qualified, and perfectly normal, a social activity. Most of the rest of us know enough to take a back seat, read and hopefully learn.

But anyone in the 'dumb money' section might compensate and turn to simple technical indicators to earn their bread and butter. .... and actually out-do the professionals. Any DVolT trader might say, "Unlike you, we don't have educated conclusions. We may have only a limited understanding of exactly how the Fed works. We have few investment opinions to defend or debate. We are suspicious of any market predictions, no matter the source. What we DO have, for an overall understanding of where the market is heading, is the slope of the 20-week moving average on a SPY chart, together with its 3-week moving average intersections. If we have no idea where the DJIA will be by New Years (and neither do YOU!) we do have a very clear picture of where it is trending right now."

They can argue, *"You DVolT investors have no curiosity what is coming up ahead. You don't even attempt to guess. If all you care about is the 'right now', whenever market trends begin to change you will ALWAYS start on the wrong side of the fence."*

And to that charge, they are correct! We will almost always be zigging when any part of the market begins to zag because guesses are treacherous. Still, however we are positioned, we will always be riding a deep-volatility pony. Our losses will be small because we will be nimble. No stubborn ego or opinion will ever persuade us to remain for long on the wrong side of market shifts – and we trade only when there's a darn good reason. That's how we roll, Joel.

DVolT accepts losses; SMALL ones while seeking longer and bigger gains. We don't know how or when market trends will change, but we're always watching and ready.

---------------.

MEMO from *The Stock Trader's Notebook: Ancient Roman soothsayers used to foretell the future by reading chicken guts. Today's television nabobs love making predictions where the market will be in six months, but modern use of poultry innards is generally frowned upon. Who knows what these guys use now? They're almost as prescient as the Romans were.*

What About Gold?

Precious metal investing has broken more faithful hearts than the Chicago Cubs. It was going to be our salvation when the eroding dollar inflated and crashed us into another Weimar Germany-type depression. Since the gold heydays of the 1970s, the big precious metals kahuna has been coming, always coming, for, oh, about a half century now. Several times in recent decades gold has gone up and up, only to collapse right back down again. Gold was going to be a great diversifier, the great hedge against bear markets, against high times and poor times It's been none of those things. It's been a bust.

Will gold ever have its day? Never say never, I suppose. You might check ASA, GOAU, GDMN, NEM, GLTR or even SLV (silver) on your longer range chart once a month or so. Meanwhile don't pawn granny's tiara and don't hold your breath.

--------------------.

Investing is the intersection of economics and psychology. --Seth Klarman

--------------------.

Cell Phone Tortures

I've never liked trading on my cell phone, though I know lots of guys do it. It's not that android investment apps are often watered down and even crude compared to working on your PC. Many android apps permit the option of working within the same appearance format you're accustomed to on Windows, albeit really tiny and at somewhat slower speed. My objection: I just dislike serious investment work on such a small screen. If I'm on my cell phone and considering a trade, I sense an added dimension of stress – the concern I may be making some sort of fat-thumb blunder or mis-read of tiny print.

OK, I'd make a trade on my Android phone if I felt it was really important and time was pressing, but the situation has never yet arisen. Nevertheless if I'm away from home for the entire day, I do like to run through my biggest positions; it's a habit.

There are several apps out there which claim to do charting graphics, but I find most of them clumsy and time-consuming. The least bad android app I've found for efficient charting is **StockSpy**, which allows you to quickly run through your biggest positions on your choice of charts with P-SAR and a single moving average which you can apply as your default. Set up the chart style you like once and you're done. Nevertheless I should add if you find yourself constantly checking positions on your cell phone, that might indicate you're becoming trade-obsessive, a red-flag danger sign.

Bow-wows and WIIW?

Suppose one day you stumble across a high dividend stock or fund and, well, against your better judgment, you are smitten. You love it. True, maybe that chart is more volatile than you'd like, but you're certain its prospects are bright and it is earning well.

Right from the start, you're violating the cardinal rule: you're developing an opinion. But you WANT this stock and that juicy yield and DVolT can go stuff it.

OK, tiger. Let's work something out. The first task, of course, is to set up your chart with the indicators you like and ---- sure enough, say the stock is trending bearish; a real Ursa Major on your plate. Now you <u>know</u> not to go for it. And that's a good thing. No matter how convinced you are, the market knows better and we always account for the old WIIW question: _What If I'm Wrong?_ So long as it is dropping you're Superman and it's Kryptonite. No arguments. The days you resent your charts the worst are the times you need them most. So you watch.... and you <u>watch</u> while your lovely stock drops … and drops. Got it?

A moment of thought should suffice. Say Torrid Teacups, Inc. is a great company; it's profitable and growing and increasing its dividend – and it's been dropping like a stone. Why would you possibly want to buy it at 24 when it's heading toward 22? What is such a hurry that you can't wait and watch for a floor? Why must you buy now? Nevertheless you're a hard case. You insist on owning this dog, so be sure you know what you will do when you it's yours.

Let's say it eventually finds support. In a few days you get your first buy signal. (So what? You get new signals every week on this roller coaster.) You buy. Time passes and one of three things occur: the stock zooms up and you get your confirming buy signal, or it stays at a rough plateau, or it turns into a headfake and melts, reversing your original moving averages "buy" signal to "sell".

There's no fourth possibility.

Now, you know when you get that new "sell" signal, you have to bail, Gail. Nothing to discuss. But if you still have a jones for this little beast, we part company right here. I dislike this stock for its volatility and for its trend But more than that, I dislike it because YOU like it so much. Suspicions of our opinions is our primo rule and you're breaking it, so I say sell. But you love Torrid Teacups and determine to hold. So as far as this stock is concerned, you and I are done. No more lectures.. Ride with it, enjoy the yield and good luck. Even the wildest mustangs work out at times. Who knows?

------------------.

MEMO from *Stock Trader's Notebook:* Love is blind. One day you forget everything to run out to buy this crazy-volatile stock and hold it for that boffo dividend (or for whatever) through hell or high water, and the devil and plagues of locusts can take your stupid DVolT signals. Look, I get it. Just don't ever buy too much, OK?

--------------------.

And the plateau scenario? You know it's not going to keep for long. You must get that "sell" or a confirming "buy" order eventually. If the latter, good. I surely hope you don't buy more and you darn well know the reason why. But we're a busted couple on this issue so .... be happy. If that little cuss surprises everyone and starts ripping upward .....well, we've been here before. You're supposed to do absolutely nothing. DVolT can't be right all the time. All I'm asking is to acknowledge to yourself that you ARE breaking your rules and you ARE determined to own the consequences. What you do off the reservation, you do deliberately, not carelessly. As ever, when discipline fails, sense of self is paramount.

Coathook Conundrums

You own a fund which has been behaving too sweetly to be true; chugging upward slow and steady. Eventually it stalls out and hits resistance and slips back a little. You trigger a SELL signal. (*Bada-Bing*) Of course you sell. But imagine the fund then stops slipping and holds in place for a while and you start to draw a "coat hook" chart. You already have a nice gain and the fund is sold. But you still like it and you watch it. Can you re-purchase it? Yes you can, but <u>only if it stops its brief</u>

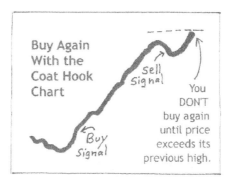

<u>little drop and climbs again to another **new high!**</u>

No arguments. You don't budge until your li'l darling reaches higher than before. Period.

But How Much Should I Use For My DVolT Trading?

I knew sooner or later we'd come to a "that depends" question, and we finally found one. If you're a college kid speculating in your dorm room with a $4000 portfolio, I'd say start with half into DVolT. If you're a stay-at-home mom with the time and inclination to follow your charts every day and you have $20,000 at your disposal, I'd say start trading maybe $4000 and leave the rest in cash or shorter term bonds for a couple of months until you're confident of your ability.

For anyone with a $50,000 portfolio and up, there are all kinds of theories to consider. You might divide your wealth up into several "buckets" and deploy each in a different way. One bucket might go into a Pimco CEF like PDO, PDI, or PTY, another into a real estate fund like JRI, one farm land fund (FPI, LAND), one in a dividend stock fund like DVY or or SDIV or a mixed fund (AOM), perhaps one in a preferred stock fund (HPS, DFP, FPF, NPFD, PFFR) maybe something in energy (XOM, BGR, OXY, KYN), and the last one, of course, in DVolT trading.

However you divide your portfolio, it is important you keep track of how well each "bucket" is doing. If, as I suspect, you do become serious about DVolT and that bucket starts to outpace all the others, well, you'll have some serious thinking to do about adjusting allocations. As discussed earlier, I'm not a big fan of diversification, but I'm still cautious enough to worry about an "all-my-eggs-in-one-basket" thing --- no matter how pretty the basket. You can refer to authors Andrew Tobias or Suze Orman for sensible ideas on allocations in setting up your account. Most major brokerages have departments devoted to helping investors to allocate their resources and apply future dividends and deposits. Trading DVolT is a learned skill, a personal journey. Minimize your risk! Never forget to begin trading in very small quantities.

Heck, even I use only a part of my money for DVolT – and I wrote the book.

-----------------------------.

MEMO from *The Stock Trader's Notebook:* We repeat – If you do decide to try DVolT for yourself, you MUST begin with testing and paper-trading for practice, and if you do begin real trading, <u>you MUST start with very small amounts.</u> Don't be crazy, Daisy.

------------------------------.

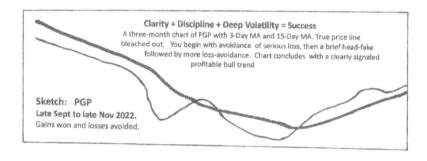

Clarity + Discipline + Deep Volatility = Success
A three-month chart of PGP with 3-Day MA and 15-Day MA. True price line bleached out. You begin with avoidance of serious loss, then a brief head-fake followed by more loss-avoidance. Chart concludes with a clearly signaled profitable bull trend

Sketch: PGP
Late Sept to late Nov 2022.
Gains won and losses avoided.

------------------------------.

A true story

Some folks seem to be natural stock pickers. They read a few articles, jot down a couple of numbers from a quarterly report, glance at a chart and land right in another honey pot – one after the other. It's uncanny sometimes. You ask them how they do it and they say something that seems beyond stupid like, "Oh, I just try to pick good stocks" or "You gotta look for companies that you understand." To hear them just increases your frustration. I'd hate 'em if I didn't admire them so much.

One guy I know – nice fella – we'll call him Alex. He once offered to pay me money if I'd sit down with him and talk about stock trading. I refused any money, of course, but I steered him to the Tobias book and said I'd be glad to talk when he finished reading it. I thought I'd never hear about it again. But a week later he'd finished "Everything You Need to Know..." and was fairly like to bust to hear more about trading. Well, our wives were close friends and we'd see each other at barbecues or some party or other and inevitably we'd get around to the market. I'll say this for him; he was smart as hell and a good listener.

Finally one day I asked where he had his money now. "In Roper," he said.

"In Roper Technologies?"

"Yeah, Roper. Where I work. I've been there for years."

"Where else?" I asked.

"Just Roper," he said.

"You mean your entire life savings and your career are all in one company?"

"Yes. So what?" So I explained to him about the theory of too much (career and life savings) all riding on one enterprise. It's generally considered prudent to spread risk around a little, I said. But that night I went to my computer and saw ROP had climbed from around 42 in 2009 to well above 400, once recently approaching 500.

I can't understand why he asked.

-----------------------------.

MEMO from *The Stock Trader's Notebook:* You don't make money by trading, you make it by sitting. It takes patience to wait for the trade to develop, for the opportunity to present itself. Let the market come to you, instead of chasing the

**market. Chart patterns are very accurate. They have proven
their accuracy and predictability time and time again, but you
have to wait for them to develop.**

— Fred McAllen, <u>Charting and Technical Analysis</u>

-----------------.

Upping Your Game

Nothing is wrong with Yahoo! Charts. For clarity and ease of
use, I love working with 'em. But if you ever feel you want to try a
more sophisticated charting system, you should take a serious look
at **thinkorswim.com** which TDAmeritrade makes available either
as a part of its online broker services or as a stand-alone paper-
trading suite for you to use at no cost. And what a platform it is!
There's more here than our DVolT system requires, but everything
thinkorswim does, they do beautifully. Here you can try out some
really exotic market indicator systems like the Haiken Ashi or the
Renko and dozens of others, but I wouldn't suggest using some of
them with real money.

Let's do a DVolT set-up on thinkorswim.com. (You're going to
be <u>very</u> happy with it.) We'll go step by step. Follow me in order.

After you have downloaded a free thinkorswim paper-trading
suite onto your PC or Apple, you start:

CLICK on CHARTS near the top of the page.

Look along the top for the little round gear wheel symbol.
CLICK on it.

Then CLICK on APPEARANCE. Scroll down to <u>Chart Type</u>
and Click on AREA. (You're getting rid of the candlestick pattern
which, as we've discussed earlier, puts out too much information
clutter. You neither need nor want it for DVolT.)

A tiny little colored box appears. CLICK on it and select a color you like.

I prefer a dull medium blue, which seems pleasing to my eye and contrasts nicely with the indicators I am about to add, but suit your own taste. Exit the APPEARANCE box by clicking on "APPLY and then click on "OK".

Now you are back to your main chart. Click again on the "Gear" symbol to return to SETTINGS. Then click on TIME AXIS. For our sample, click on TIME INTERVAL of "6 months" and AGGREGATION PERIOD of "Two days". Then click on APPLY and on OK to exit.

Stay with me here! Once back to your main chart, find the little half-full "Chemical Beaker" symbol for "STUDIES". You'll see a column of different technical indicators on the left. Scroll down to find good ol' **PARABOLIC SAR**. CLICK on it. Then click ADD SELECTED. Then click on APPLY. Then click on OK.

Don't wimp out on me now! **This last one is <u>very</u> important.** Return to STUDIES by clicking again on the Chemical Beaker. Scroll down the list to find **PPS**. Click on it. Then click on ADD SELECTED. Click on APPLY, and exit by clicking on OK. (Whew!)

Congratulations. You're done.

Say hello to my little friend: your new world-class technical trading suite

Let's talk about what you've just created. Since you chose "Two Days" as your aggregation period, (similar to "Interval Period" on Yahoo) you have already pre-smoothed out your chart to reduce daily market noise. No need to bleach anything out or clutter up your chart with moving average overlays. You already applied the **PPS** (Persons Pivot Study) which incorporates two moving averages (one slow, the other fast) already built in. PPS was developed by John Persons, a brilliant trader/analyst and – to my mind – it works superbly with DVolT. See for yourself. Punch in MMT, or AOM or any other DVolT trading asset on your new thinkorswim chart and see how effectively those PPS up and down arrows signal the trend that immediately follows.

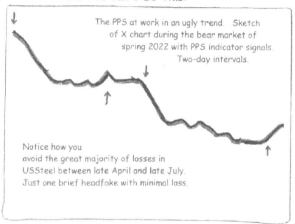

Don't Tell Me You Can't Do This:

The PPS at work in an ugly trend. Sketch of X chart during the bear market of spring 2022 with PPS indicator signals. Two-day intervals.

Notice how you avoid the great majority of losses in USSteel between late April and late July. Just one brief headfake with minimal loss.

Notice also on the sketch how the P-SAR and the PPS usually work together. Whenever you see one indicator change, the other promptly changes with it or just a couple of days later. This gives you a hint on how you might proceed with your money management plan. Suppose you decide a $5000 buy is a "half intended position" and $10,000 will be your "full intended position" on any stock you will hold. Now imagine your MMT is in a bearish trend, then one day you see a P-SAR "buy" signal. You immediately buy a "half" position or $5000 worth, but you do not buy more until the PPS confirms your first signal and also flashes a "Buy" arrow. When you see the second BUY signal, you immediately add from a half position to a full allocation. But if you never see the confirming signal, if MMT gives you a quick headfake and the "AVOID" PSAR re-appears instead, then you sell your half position and your losses are minimized.

But there are exceptions to the usual PPS and P-SAR agreement, especially when a volatile stock makes sharp moves. Below is a sketch of American Airlines (AA) chart action in early 2022 and, at the very start, see the two signals once failed to synchronize for three days on a big downward movement. Nothing is perfect in this business.

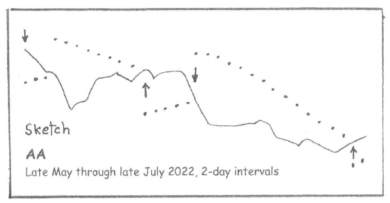

Sketch

AA

Late May through late July 2022, 2-day intervals

A not-entirely satisfying chart of a not-entirely Lo-Vol stock. The PPS and the P-SAR frequently (but not always) work closely in harness. Note in May the chart begins with a SELL signal from the PPS, but the P-SAR stays bullish during several ugly trading days before it too signals SELL. This is why we sell aggressively on the first bear signal. It is also why AA is too volatile for LoVolT trading.

---------------.

MEMO from *The Stock Trader's Journal*: If I had to use just one indicator on one chart using strictly DVolT assets, I would use the PPS on thinkorswim's 3-month chart with a two-day aggregation.

If you remain with Yahoo! as your technical suite, moving averages, perhaps coupled with P-SAR, is probably the best combo you're going to get, and it's a very good one. If you're comfortable using it, there's no compelling reason to change. But if I had my druthers, I'd prefer to use thinkorswim.com just so I could put PPS into my mix.

Watching multiple different charts working independently on the same screen.

Thinkorswim has you covered.

Go to your chart page and direct your attention to the extreme upper right corner of your computer screen. Wa-a-a-y up over there, not far from the "Chemical Beaker" symbol, you will see a small empty rectangle. CLICK on it and you will see a large box made up of 48 very little boxes.

By dragging your mouse you can highlight two or three or four or six or any number of boxes you choose. CLICK on the highlighted boxes and you now have a full page with as many different chart boxes as you want. Set up each chart as differently as you like. I like to work with three boxes continuously visible on the same screen; a one month, a three-month and a 6-month chart, each overlaid with the P-SAR and PPS technical indicators. For the one-month I use One-Day Aggregation, but for the 3-month or 6-month chart I use the 2-day Aggregation. (For a 9-month chart, I would smooth it all the way out to a 3-day Aggregation, but that's as far out in smoothing as I will ever go.) If you will do this set-up, or something similar, Voila! -- there you'll have it – all your charts will continue to operate as you have set them up and will work independently from each other. For all intents and purposes you now work with a thinkorswim professional-level chart trading suite linked to TDAmeritrade that is simple, clear and darned effective.

And nuthin' beats free, Marie.

The "Upcoming Big Event" Dilemma: A Little Case Study

The date: November 1, 2022. The entire investing world awaited Fed Chairman Powell's scheduled remarks after resetting interest rates. Everyone anticipated a 75- basis point hike. That was a given. But looking ahead, would Powell signal a possible softening of subsequent rate hikes? Or would he give the markets a Fed-speak tongue-lashing threat of more aggressive hikes to come? No one knew if the recent job growth numbers would convince the Fed to tighten the thumb screws another couple of notches or if fear of causing a recession would cajole them into softening their tone.

Within my accounts, my three-month thinkorswim chart (with 2-day aggregation) had recently thrown off a good PPS "Buy" signal, confirmed by a new bullish P-SAR pattern for AOM and I had bought a very large position just the previous week on October 25. As ever, the question was "NOW what?" All my signals were bullish, yet I knew (we ALL knew!) Powell's remarks could trigger a violent market move and there was no way of telling which way the jolt would go. Oh, you could have an opinion, of course – but remember avoiding opinions is at the heart of what we do with DVolT.

From where I sat, I could take a nice little 2% gain for the week, selling before the Nov. 1st close or I could ride the lightening as Powell would speak on the 2nd.

I sold.

------------------.

MEMO from *The Stock Trader's Notebook:* We demand probabilities. Coin-toss odds are never good enough. When I face an exceptionally big and violent market event with an unknowable outcome, I go mostly to cash. For me, wealth preservation must always come first.

----------------.

What Time To Check?

If you are using moving average crossovers for your signals it probably doesn't much matter what time of day you check your charts, though I do like working one consistent time of day, every day. Using P-SAR or PPS signals is a little different. Several times I have seen markets make a big early morning move and have signals pop up, only to have the market reverse itself and the signals disappear the same afternoon! That is why I try to check my charts daily between about 3:00 and 3:30 or so. If you're working during those hours, setting a few minutes aside on your lunch break will have to do. I would discourage mornings, but any time is better than not checking your positions at all.

Success breeds complacency.
Complacency breeds failure.
Only the paranoid survive.
--Andrew Grove

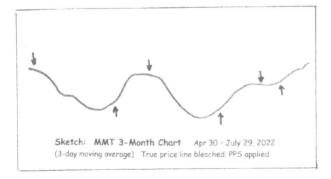

Sketch: MMT 3-Month Chart   Apr 30 - July 29, 2022
(3-day moving average)   True price line bleached. PPS applied

Out on the Edge

The MFS Multimarkets Income Trust (Symbol: MMT) is another fund with a chart history pattern that has approached my ideal for DVolT trading. I have little idea how the little critter might behave in the future, of course, but so far it has been so profitable to trade that I almost regret calling attention to it. I've sketched out a recent three-month chart of its 2-day moving average hugging the true price line which I've bleached out for clarity and, well, it practically begs you to make a profit. Notice the PPS signals I have penned in; you have six of them. Five are nicely profitable and one we could call a minimal loss head-fake.

If a casino manager caught a blackjack player regularly winning five out of six hands, he'd call security to roust the bum out the door, but here with DVolT charts applied, you win and win and no one notices.

Again: we repeat the tactic according to our DVolT rules. You hold your MMT position for as long as both your indicators are bullish, but when just ONE of them changes to "Sell" you immediately unload either 2/3 or even all your position in MMT, and probably take profits right there. If you sold 2/3 of MMT on your first "sell" signal, you promptly dump the rest as soon as you see the confirming bearish indication. As before, I have found I do better if I make a habit of selling more aggressively than I buy on the theory assets can frequently drop faster than they climb.

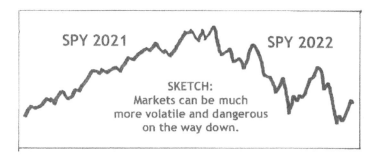

SPY 2021   SPY 2022

SKETCH:
Markets can be much
more volatile and dangerous
on the way down.

The MAMI Chart – Minimal Attention, Minimal Involvement

--For investors who hate trading

FIRST: Go to Yahoo Charts, enter AOM and click on ONE YEAR

SECOND: Bleach out the true price line, as shown before

THIRD: Under INDICATORS, click MOVING AVERAGES and change 50 to 3

FOURTH: Return to INDICATORS, click on MOVING AVERAGES and change 50 to 20. Be sure your moving average lines are different colors.

FIFTH: Change INTERVAL from 1D to 1W

SIXTH: Add P-SAR

And you are done. You now have a free but effective technical system which will direct you to trade only a few times a year. Let's take a look at how it works:

The SLOPE of your 20-Week Line gives you a good idea of the kind of market you are in. So long as it slopes DOWNWARD or is more or less FLAT, you want to be especially cautious. You can be ambitious only when your 20-Line slopes unmistakably upward.

Buy a modest position in AOM if you have a flattish 20-Line but the 3-Line is above it and sloping upward.

Buy a LARGE position when you have a 20WMA UPWARD SLOPE and a Bullish Crossover.

Whatever you own, you HOLD it until the moment your 3-Line crosses below your 20-Line Then you SELL.

On a DVolT "minimal trading" six-month chart the P-SAR gives you a second indicator – to hold, to avoid, to buy or to sell. The six month chart with two moving averages deals in broad strokes and will not protect you much if you try it with volatile funds or stocks that hit a sudden bear market. If you wish to keep the P-SAR, use it only as an added confirmation; as your secondary tool.

------------.

Long story short:

Be fully invested in AOM when 20-Line is flat or rising AND 3-Line is above it.

Be mostly in cash when 20-Line is falling OR when 3-Line is below it.

And when we say MAMI is "minimal involvement" we mean just that. TOTL, AOM, long or short, or TLT with TBF are the only assets you might trade. You are either fully in or totally into cash or shorter term bonds.

(Now is that so hard?)

--------------.

In our chart sketch below, we use AOM in a generally bear market. We start with a decent gain then are out of a falling market. Around April with have a short false rally which turns into a minimal loss head-fake, and we end with a strong likelihood of a bull rally. We didn't make much, but we really avoided big losses while the market was dropping hard.

Remember: For the clearest overall view, Step back, WAY back ---

Set Up: Yahoo! Finance TWO YEAR chart with 10-WEEK and 40-Week moving averages on 1W intervals. From these perspectives, market directions become almost unmistakable.

And now I repeat my caveat. There is a potential price you pay for minimal attention/minimal involvement. If portfolio protection is an important reason why we use DVolT in the first place, charts like this are second-best tools. Their signals are just too slow to fully protect your portfolio upon the onset of any but slower bearish trends.

-------------------.

"Don't worry about what the markets are going to do, worry about what you are going to do in response to the markets. " Michael Carr

-------------------.

Yes, I know. People will argue they are uncomfortable with even twice a year trading. But I'm not presenting this system to make them comfortable. I'm presenting it to make them successful – and to avoid serious loss you simply must trade on timely signals. If you set up your one-year chart just as described with the 3-Week and the 20-Week Moving Averages and you confine your charting for a $50,000 position in only AOM, very likely months will go by before you are required to make a trade. For reluctant, infrequent traders, that small compromise is best I can offer and still be effective.

Like the man said, investing isn't back rubs.

Below: another far-back perspective look of general market trends in a two-year SPY chart.

------------------.

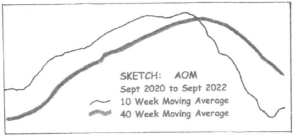

For a Better Perspective, Use Two-Year Charts

SKETCH: AOM
Sept 2020 to Sept 2022
10 Week Moving Average
40 Week Moving Average

You enjoyed a long climb and avoided a long, ugly fall.
Conclusion: AOM is recovering. You may now buy a small
position only, but wait for MA cross for any large investment.

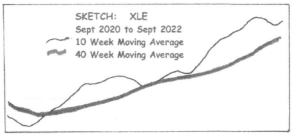

SKETCH: XLE
Sept 2020 to Sept 2022
10 Week Moving Average
40 Week Moving Average

Conclusion: Energy is volatile but still bullish. You have good
gains and further gains look favorable. Continue to hold.

A Final Word: We call him Mr. Market because he rules

Even if you fancy yourself a fairly active trader on shorter term signals, you should never lose track of the overall market trend as you will instantly see by returning to a MAMI chart now and then. I'm not now saying near the end of this book that you should ignore your signals (!) – but rather you should always be clear which way the tide is running. Say you have already decided that your maximum allocation in any one stock or fund will never exceed $10,000. Say also you get good bullish signals on BRK-B when you know darn well the overall market is trending bearish. What to do? Buy your BRK-B, yes, but make your buy smaller than you otherwise might and certainly don't plan on owning more than say, half of your usual maximum allocation. And watch that position like a hawk.

Don't fight the tape.

On the other hand ----

It would probably be wrong of me to finish this book without even mentioning some ideas if you are determined to buy and hold and D-Vol+T trading isn't for you. So, distilled from the nay-sayers and counter arguments, you might consider.....

BRK-B It's the real deal; Buffet's very own Berkshire Hathaway. Further comment unnecessary.

AOM A reasonable mix of stocks and bonds in one fund. AOM is part stocks and the rest bonds. Tracks SPY quite closely, but with a quieter chart. A fund for the moderately cautious. Also consider AOK, TOTL, DVY, NUSI or SDIV, a global equity fund with big dividends.

PFE An ETF of preferred stocks & income. Nice steady yield but modest upside, possibly. Also DFP

PTY Maybe the most famous closed end bond fund of them all. A reputation for astute management. Really big distributions in its history, but also a good share of ups and downs. Also watch PDI, PDO, PAXS, DSL.

FPI We read Bill Gates has been investing heavily into productive farmland. You might too. Also consider DBMF, LAND or hospitals with MPW.

KYN Energy infrastructure closed end fund. Pipelines etc. Good distributions. MEGI is a possible alternative.

XOM Exxon won't bankrupt you. An energy Big Kahuna with good dividend stream. Consider also BGR or OXY.

MUA Municipal bond CEF for income and reduced taxes. Also VMO and NBH

JRI A global real estate income and growth fund

GNT Mix of energy and precious metals exposure in a closed end fund.

... and many more, of course, each with its own potential benefits and risks. If you have many years ahead of you and don't want to trade actively, you should Google "dollar cost averaging" especially with SPY or DVY. Being young with a big future is a great advantage. Don't forget to look into I-Bonds! Good luck.

And now -- a word from the opposition

I have to confess I know an intelligent person or two claiming to have run back-tests on DVolT theory, showing that another method is more profitable. They say my thinking needs to be "more robust", that my success is merely "anecdotal".... even that readers can't replicate my success with D-VolT.

Well, you just might, Dwight. I think you can do this. Even the critics I know won't actually say DVolT is dangerous, ineffective or unmanageable or will lose money - just that some other method is better. As a for instance, they give me -- you guessed it -- buy-and-hold! And so we come full circle back to nay-sayers.

I well know what often happens to buy-and-hold when emotions rage as savings melt away and distraught innocents lose their nerve in market panics. I know what happens when some poor half-informed rookie clings to a falling stock because of its unrealistic dividend. But for some people, maybe the nay-sayers are right after all. In the end, maybe it's really better for some to just own an index fund like SPY -- maybe to stay blissfully unaware -- have minimal interest in the stock market. You might focus on your job, your family and other interests while shoveling money into a market index 401k with nary a thought of how you or the world is doing... because if you DO pay attention to markets, and if you DON'T deploy something like DVolT, your emotions and opinions WILL work on you.

In the past, long term buy-and-hold worked splendidly, as we have seen. But -- we ask again -- NOW what? If the past is indeed prelude and vast economic tides persist for future decades, then you have some advantage to be confident with "staying the course". After all, we've already established how unnerving a habit of watching stock market news reports can be. And we DO know how treacherous emotions can be in a crash when portfolios are smashed like roadkill and a million weeping investors are scurrying about like their hair's on fire. Maybe for the rest of your life the DJIA really will keep on recovering higher and higher after every bear market. It always has! If someone locks you away in a closet for twenty years, who knows how rich you might be when you get out?

So I could indeed be wrong. But I don't think so. If broad index buy-and-hold proves superior to DVolT or some other flexible tactic in the coming years, and if we are looking ahead to another happy, bullish era, then I believe you MIGHT wind up with somewhat less using DVolT than you might have otherwise. But those are two big "ifs". We may well face economic storms ahead, and I believe DVolT or other plan could rescue you from grave calamity.

Look -- I'm into my 70s now -- an age when one's little tics and stupid habits and weaknesses are like old guests that never leave the party. Personally speaking, I feel certain I'm better to exit a position when the market is just starting to crumble rather than to risk the tornado's full wrath. But hey -- that's me. Maybe you're made of sterner stuff. Some folks are, I know.

MEMO from *The Stock Trader's Notebook:* **In the end, when the chin music's all been played, no one knows nothin' about the market's future -- except that it will change. Bank on it.**

Discipline and Character

I long ago decided that attempting to apply DVolT had something to do with developing character. When I see an upward sloping chart stall, dip a bit and then start to trend upward again higher, and when its indicator repeats its earlier BUY signal, almost always my inclination is to wait and watch "just a day or two maybe" to see if the renewed trend will really take. But that's just fear talking. Or suppose you've spotted a DVolT stock that, after a long, painful drop, is finally bouncing upward off its support price. We can surmise that its chance of reversing downward again may be about the same the third day of its new bullish trend as its eighth day, or its twentieth. On any particular day that DVolT stock's likelihood of reversing downward is probably less than 50/50, but the accumulation of those less-than-likely days adds up to a certainty. One day it WILL drop. And although that day is unknown, the longer you wait to buy, the closer you are to the end of the bullish trend.. My logic is that it's best for you to hit the BUY trigger as soon as you're able -- (small buy on your first signal and a larger buy when you get confirmation). But I've never gotten over that feeling I should wait and see. Even after long experience in DVolT, when that new trade signal pops up on the far right edge of my chart, a flush of doubt inevitably follows.

The same inner fears and doubts may be blocking you from effective, probability-based decisions too. Those jitters may even be hard wired into our psyches, the psychological echoes of ancient caveman anxieties and suspicions at work. It didn't pay our hominid forebears to be careless about risk. Say it's 100,000 BC and you and your miserable flea bitten little tribe are huddled around a wretched fire as darkness falls. No one sees more than a few yards into the vast darkness that surrounds you.

Someone hears soft movement out in the tall grass. Of course you leap to your feet, grab your club and grunt the alarm. The sound you heard could be from anything – a rabbit, a zebra or a jackal sniffing about for a discarded bone. The chance that it's a big cat stalking your little camp is actually quite slim. There are a lot of other critters out there. But it didn't pay for Early Man on the edge of extinction to play probabilities. He had little to gain if it was only a rabbit out there, but very much to lose if a lioness. For Mr. 100,000 BC, every unseen movement in the darkness had to be regarded as a terrible threat. Never forget that he and all our ancestors for hundreds of thousands of years shaped the twitchy, often illogical brains we now use to trade equities in the 21st century. Genetics has a long memory and a powerful grip.

------------.

There is only one way to stay wealthy; some combination of frugality and paranoia and that's a topic we don't discuss enough. Getting money requires taking risks and being optimistic but keeping money requires the opposite of taking risk, it requires humility; fear that what you've made can be taken away from you. It requires frugality and an acceptance that some of what you made is attributable to luck. --**Morgan Housel, The Psychology of Money**

-------------.

Psychologists studying investors tell us that the pain of losing is often more intense than the pleasure of winning a profit. That too I believe is an echo from our hunter-gatherer past. The pleasure some early man must have enjoyed when coming across a four-day old elk carcass lying in the hot sun must have been somewhat less than the terror of a pursuit by a lion. So when today's investor, the mental and emotional heir of knuckle-dragging ancestors, suddenly sees that promising "hockey stick curve" on a downward sloping chart that appears to be changing direction upwards, his caveman brain – ever suspicious and doubtful – tugs at him not to act, to wait a bit and maybe watch to see what happens tomorrow.

--------------------.

But we are born-again DVolT investors. We've studied and practiced, and it is happy consequences that we seek, for they are beyond possible; with proper trading discipline they become even probable. We have a rudimentary understanding of odds. We can mentally balance possible losses against potential gains and can will ourselves to trade selectively despite the unruly emotions and inclinations bequeathed to us. We know that optimal opportunity moments are fleeting. Early humans had very few happy alarms. For them, surprises were dreadful, even fatal. So for us, when confronted with a moment fraught with incomplete knowledge, it is deep in our instincts to want to pause, to listen, to know more.

And that's where character comes in. We know all about the scoffers and the "It can't be done" arguments, but with practice, I believe we might overcome suspicions. When the trading moment does arrive, when that DVolT line curves gently upward and the PPS signal pops up on the far right edge of your thinkorswim chart, you really may feel fear and the desire to hesitate despite the favorable graphics right in front of you. But with a little determination, you might make that first disciplined DVolT "half allocation buy" anyway. Guts may have something to do with it – but I think it's more a matter of informed discipline to manage risks and opportunities. If you make the disciplined trade, congratulations. You're in the game. Another wise guy finds his moxie.

Students of buyer psychology tell us at a certain point, when varieties of products on supermarket shelves become overabundant, the consumer's dilemma of choosing just one becomes more difficult, not less. It's hardly a stretch to imagine that the investor trying to choose among thousands of funds and stocks faces a similar problem. Any equity s/he buys will almost inevitably be bested by many others.

Suppose however you greatly reduced your range of choices by a process that made excellent sense to you. Once you have trimmed your investment choices down to a particular few stocks and funds that share one highly unusual but valuable quality, you're no longer paralyzed with anxiety or indecision caused by choice overload. You discover why you have good reason to focus on VFMV, AOM and TOTL instead of hundreds of other funds. Your road ahead becomes clearer. You become empowered with the clarity.

Also consider the DVolT method gives you a clearly specified path for holding or exiting any position. You are never again stymied by the fretful when-to-sell question when markets are in motion.

True, in a bull market many funds will move more profitably than DvolT securities, but how many will also give you a realistic opportunity to gain when markets turn bearish? How many funds give you a realistic fighting chance to deploy trading tactics and profit by playing both sides of the long/short bull/bear coin as with TLT and TBF? You know the answer: almost none.

---------------.

Life is not about finding yourself. Life is about creating yourself. — Lolly Daskal

---------------.

And now there's one last angle to examine. Keep in mind the effect of the <u>location</u> any new signal can have on your emotions. Consider: in learning DVolT trading theory you may look at a hundred charts. You will be able to examine the places various signals appeared and you can follow what happened immediately afterwards. In actuality you're following little histories of chart behavior. "Yes, I see," you might say to yourself. "The sell signal popped up HERE and then I see the DVolT fund continued to fall."

Or you might say, "Aha! The signal flashed HERE and then the chart did THAT...." You might (and should!) observe again and again, studying chart after chart as you practice the DVolT protocol and gain in confidence, deciding for yourself whether probabilities are truly in your favor. These accumulated stories are all very comforting and encouraging; the more you study charts and indicators on select assets, the better you may finally decide for yourself if DVolT is a worthwhile plan for you.

But no one wants to be a student forever. Eventually you may want to make a real investment, and if you do, there will be a critical difference in any new chart you examine. You can't trade in the past where the outcome is already written. You trade in the present. You trade in the NOW. And in all DVolT trades you must focus at the critical point of any chart, <u>the extreme right edge</u>, the part where there is no "and then" to see. The far right edge of any chart with its MA cross-overs, or PPS or P-SAR indicators is your last "let's get serious" point, your action nexus. The rest of your chart may show you whether that stock or fund even belongs on your D-VolT list, but that's not where you make your choice. Once you are confident your chart indeed shows a workable DVolT pattern, then your eye should immediately focus over on the now point, the jump-off point – the right edge where real life decisions are made. And don't let yourself be distracted at decision time. Remember there was a reason why we did everything we could do to slim down, to strip away and simplify our charts, to remove distractions and unimportant market noise and details. We did it to clarify, to eliminate the irrelevant.

OK, say it's 3:30 PM. Your new PPS "buy" signal has been sitting there, on the extreme right side of your three-month DVolT chart all day and the market closes in a half hour. Rationally, you believe the fund you are about to trade will trend as you expect next week because you know how it has consistently behaved in the past. Your safest option, of course, is always to do nothing – but you're a wise guy investor, a player. You haven't come all this way to sit on your hands and opt for a 2 or 3% CD in a bank account. Nevertheless you have to decide if DVolT is worth your risk when you have investing alternatives at hand.

In the end, successful traders take managed risks, those leaps into uncertainty when they have reason to be confident the odds gods are smiling and that the risks are being managed. But not everyone is made to be a stock trader. Plenty of people are satisfied to put their money into a dividend portfolio, forget all about the market and go fishing. For all its warts, a plan to buy-and-hold a diversified portfolio of dividend stocks and corporate bonds probably isn't the worst decision you can make. So if you distrust DVolT theory as it's been explained, or if you can't – or won't -- follow a disciplined protocol that specializes in a select few securities when probabilities appear to beckon, then DO NOTHING or DO SOMETHING ELSE is probably your better course. When your finger hovers over that computer mouse and the cursor rests over the BUY button on your monitor, that's a very different matter than studying last month's chart action. You've learned the principles. You have planned your trades. Now you must test and test and trade your plans – carefully disciplined – or not.

All the best.

An Afterward:

Abe Lincoln once quoted a pastor who said, "I could write shorter sermons, but once I start I get too lazy to stop." I know how he felt.

After years writing investment commentary, the further I got into this manuscript the more fun I had. I hope you enjoyed it too, but I hope even more it gave you useful insights into some disciplined investing tactics. I'd appreciate any honest feedback or review you might send to amazon or to your book-seller. If there's ever a second edition to this book, it would be helpful to know what worked for you and how to improve the original.

Now get out there and make some money.

-Richard Smith